BECOMING INSPIRED

BECOMING INSPIRED

Srinivas Arka

Coppersun Books

Published by Coppersun Books, PO Box 2217, London W1A 5GZ, United Kingdom
Web site: www.coppersunbooks.com
Email: admin@coppersunbooks.com

Set in Garamond

ISBN 0-954541-80-4

Typeset by Edgerton Publishing Services, Pett, Hastings, UK

Printed by Antony Rowe Limited, Chippenham, UK

Contents

I **Beginnings** 1
    1 The Development of Consciousness 2
    2 Laws of the Inner and Outer Universe 8

II **Fulfilment** 15
    3 Seeking Love and Searching for Truth 16
    4 Truth 20
    5 Truth and Love 25

III **The Essence** 29
    6 Religion and Spirituality 30
    7 Experience and Illumination 35

IV **Wave of Life** 47
    8 The Smile, a Gesture of Humanity 48
    9 The Ebb and Flow of Consciousness 52
    10 Potential 57
    11 Living 61
    12 Life-Force 67

V **Light and Energy** 71
    13 Darkness and Light 72
    14 Energy and Timelessness 75
    15 The Nature and Purpose of Energy 80

VI **The Universe** 91
    16 Cosmic Evolution 92
    17 Beyond the Physical 97
    18 Journeying between the Outer and the Inner Realms . . 101

VII Nature. 105

   19 Visible and Invisible Nature 106

VIII Consciousness. 111

   20 Consciousness beyond Science. 112

   21 The Manifestation of Consciousness. 121

   22 The Experience of Consciousness. 126

IX   Space. 133

   23 Visibility and Invisibility 134

   24 Awareness of Inner Space. 140

   25 Inner and Outer Space. 147

X   Time 155

   26 The Three Folds of the Day. 156

   27 The Invisible Clock. 162

XI   The Heart. 173

   28 Natural Laws and Spiritual Advancement 174

   29 Inner and Outer Experience. 180

   30 The Progression to Enlightenment –

       A Series of Steps. 190

Glossary of Terms 199

I

BEGINNINGS

Cosmically, there are no beginnings or endings

1

The Development of Consciousness

Whether one is a child or an adult, innocence is the underlying, consistent nature at the core of all beings.

P ure spirit-consciousness is seen in newborn babies. Their small bodies carry elevated, pure spirit-consciousness that is so fresh and so cosmic that it is very closely connected with the core of universal nature. Babies are pure in their being and the consciousness that pervades them is humble and non-judgemental.

Every movement a newborn baby makes is inspired and influenced directly by nature. Gradually, the extended spirit-consciousness recedes into the heart centre as the body grows. This process creates the 'I' (the ego), a new shoot growing from pure spirit-consciousness and forming an entity that is a potential thinking faculty in the newborn, but which we later recognize as the mind. This leads to curiosity and in turn to the gaining of experience through acts of inquisitiveness and thus to the development of a natural sense of awareness. The baby's mind gradually becomes a questioning mind and shifts to a more logical pattern of thinking. The first expression from the spirit-consciousness of a new-born baby is innocence. The same can be felt in a very elderly person, when all sheaths of secondary nature such as pride, envy and greed wither away. Much of consciousness returns from the head to the heart, leading once again to the expression of innocence from the pure spirit-consciousness.

At birth, the controlling pure spirit-consciousness is prominent in the region of the heart, and spreads itself vigorously to all the layers and regions of the body. The same pure spirit-consciousness gradually manifests itself more effectively in the head on the surface of the mind, as a thinking entity with its roots reaching deeply into the brain. Mind and brain fuse together, resulting in the development of faculties such as intellect. These faculties are the most basic expression of the infinite spirit-consciousness that dwells within us, yet they cannot be ignored, because the power of the mind also has the potential and qualities of the pure spirit-consciousness that dwells predominantly in the heart. As we grow out of infancy, we begin to affirm with our rational minds that our existence is mainly physical. At this stage, pure spirit-consciousness recedes into our hearts.

As we mature, we experience the world and achieve our goals using our physical senses. Why do we need our physical senses? They are tools that help us understand the physical world. If we become totally dependent on these senses, we may not realize that we are more than we think we are. Furthermore, the information gathered from our senses can sometimes be deceptive, so that, by depending on our physical senses alone, we may live a life of only mediocre quality. However, a time may come when the deeper, feeling entity within us grows and we evolve with it so that we are no longer wholly dependent on the physical senses.

We have an inner, mystical eye. This is the mother of all our senses because it is more powerful than the physical senses. While the physical eye can only receive light, the inner eye can also hear, smell, sense and feel. We come to know this only when we experience it. The literature of research shows that there are many examples of our ability to visualize first and then transform our visualization into a physical reality. Scientists, artists and astronomers first visualize their concepts, so that they can gain a virtual experience of an aspect of nature; then they pursue this, by experimentation, with the intention of creating or discovering a reality. This reality is a substantiation of their original virtual experience. It is with this approach that the earth has been explored and minerals and other treasures have been discovered. Humankind has changed the world and will continue to make changes.

Whatever we call this inner mystical eye, intuition, precognition, or a sense of deep, though logic-denying, feeling, we still do not know what it fully is. However, we all know that it is somewhere within us. In essence, whatever we see or think or do, everything is reduced to some form of subtle feeling within us. This is emotional or feeling memory. There are animals that have fewer senses than we have; for example, bats without vision and snakes without hearing, but they still experience life to the full. *The heart is the mother of all the senses; next in importance is the mind; then all the other senses.* We move into different dimensions in consciousness, just as our galaxy is moving in space all the time. *We also journey into the cosmos, but in mystical ways, and, although these experiences are stored within our hearts, we cannot always remember them.* These mystical insights and spiritual experiences are retained in the deeper self in the form of subtle impressions, some of which are

4

remembered by the surface mind. Much is left unexpressed and unexplained. This is when we express ourselves through inspirational poetry, in an attempt to communicate experiences that are barely expressible in words.

Gestures

Our inner feelings are infinite, whereas our words are finite. This is why we usually feel dissatisfied when expressing our deeper thoughts or emotions. Even if we speak a thousand words, they will still only be a surface explanation of what we feel within. Hence, poets are at the forefront of expression. They specialize in capturing infinite concepts and encapsulating ideas into a condensed script. Our inner feelings, emotions and deeper thoughts emanate like waves from our being, overflowing the barriers of logic. If a poem is read with a purely rational mind, the reader will be disappointed and encounter only flaws and mistakes. Furthermore, we may conclude that the poem is nonsensical and has no merit. However, if we read with an unquestioning mind and a feeling heart, we discover the deeper meanings and wisdom inherent in the poem.

Mystics use various methods to convey their deepest thoughts and concepts. They use wordless tunes, for example humming sounds at varied pitch. They also use gestures, which are direct expressions of the heart. When we let our hearts speak, our hands move spontaneously or naturally making certain gestures. Mystics use these gestures to convey spiritual wisdom. The messages intuited from them can travel directly from heart to heart, unsoiled by external influences or negative forces.

Our thoughts can be conveyed to others through the use of words. However, this alone is not enough and this robotic method of verbal communication cannot convey how infinite our feelings, emotions and experiences are. A certain tone of voice has to accompany our words, while eyes, facial expressions and vibrations from the body, mind and being are all components of effective communication. As we move to subtler expression, we use certain gestures without our mind's knowledge. As our consciousness in expression deepens, we use fewer words and pour more meaning into these gestures. Here, the sentient heart takes over. These are 'mystic gestures', which articulate beyond ordinary gesticulation. They not only convey the deeper meaning intended, but also alter the states of consciousness in both the person expressing and the person absorbing the gestures' inner meanings. *Mystic gestures represent certain elements in nature that either invite or disseminate energies, and use of these gestures is a process that begins at birth.*

Babies mainly use gestures to convey their needs to their mothers in a manner that is immensely enlightening. The movement of each finger conveys a wealth of meaning to the mother; she understands the significance of each gesture, yet there is no development of vocabulary present in the baby's mind.

We are able to discern and discriminate between the past, present and future because of the nature of memory. We cannot identify the future without considering the present and the past. The process of ageing is so beautiful, graceful and mystical that we do not even realize how we are being processed through time by the universe. Loss of memory, however, does not mean total loss; instead, memories are converted into subtle impressions and automatically stored somewhere deep within the body and individual consciousness. Eventually the essence remains and the rest disappears. This can be seen in a very elderly person with dwindling memory and explicit simplicity. Once again the heart celebrates and the mind returns to a state of innocence.

Memories are transformed into the essence of deeper impressions. The cosmic spirit-consciousness, being so pure, enters the material form of existence to gain life-experiences and then moves onto higher or different planes of existence. We are all consciously and unconsciously growing and journeying. There is life everywhere and we experience this at many levels. We can experience the deeper Self if we withdraw ourselves from worldly activities for some time and remain in solitude. In this state, our excessive outgoing energies and resources are reduced and the wish to discover ourselves inspires us to *feel* the largely forgotten or ignored side of our deeper existence. At this time, some people follow their own intuitive guidance, while others simply blossom as they become aware of the newly discovered joys in their lives and their connection with nature and the universe. This process is not instantaneous. Rather, it is a gradual, elegant flowering of the inner self, with many petals representing physical, mystical and spiritual abilities.

Each of us is bound to grow and evolve at some point. There is an individual time for everyone within the universal time. Apart from our responsibility and accountability for our own growth and expansion, evolution and growth do not result only from the will of human beings but are the imperatives of the universe.

The discovery of the true Self does not happen overnight. It requires consistent effort, determination and dedication. This is a graceful and fulfilling quest, an adventure of self-discovery.

2

Laws of the Inner and Outer Universe

We are more than we think we are. We are more than we believe we are. We are more than we can imagine.

The body is a container and its content is conscious life-energy. This combination of infinite content in a finite body is a cosmic riddle, not to be solved, but to be celebrated with wonder. A thinking mind only adds confusion to this riddle, whereas a feeling heart is able to celebrate it with innocence. The more the riddle is analysed, the more complex and intricate it becomes.

As we grow and evolve, scientifically, technologically, intuitively and spiritually, we realize that the laws of the universe that govern our physical existence do not cover the whole cosmic experience. While the law of gravity is universal, its effects are different on the earth, the moon, Mars and the stars. We accept that scientific laws known by us today are not the absolute laws of the entire cosmos. Lower nature, although bound by physical laws can also be subject to higher nature. The laws of the physical body are different from the laws of the mind. The laws of the mind are different from the free-flowing emotions and feelings of the heart. The structure and beliefs of our physical life are different from the compassionate nature of the universe.

The physical world of man-made laws is constrained within the framework of society. Every human being thinks about how he or she can succeed as an individual in society. 'How can I prosper?' is the first question that is asked, while 'How can others progress?' is either a secondary question or one that is never asked. If, however, the situation is reversed and the second question is asked first, the questioning becomes a spiritual inquiry and individual progress becomes peripheral to the course of expanding collective consciousness. 'How can I progress?' is a common question focused on an individual's self-growth. The notion 'Let me be happy' is in conformity with the laws of the mind and the laws of physical existence. 'Let others be happy' is a wish born out of a spiritual heart. When a person worries only about himself or herself, their connection with the world becomes weak.

We can only be truly happy when others around us are happy. However, with the limited laws of the rational mind, this concept is usually reversed and becomes 'If I am happy, then others may be happy too', which is significantly different. It does not aspire to truth. *The realization and experience of one's spirituality become possible when the universe and all beings in it are comprehended as a single, whole entity. Such an understanding and experience of wholeness raises one's consciousness towards enlightenment.*

One rises to heights of consciousness when the mind is turned inward so that the very laws of the cosmos and of consciousness can be understood and felt deeply. Consciousness cannot be heightened when one is floating on the surface. Only when we have discovered the very roots of our consciousness do we achieve deeper awareness. However, such awareness requires patience and endurance.

Why do we have a such a strong tendency to close our eyes when we see either an unpleasant scene or one of great beauty? In both cases our eyes close unconsciously for a moment. When we want to reject something outside of ourselves that does not support or encourage our existence or well-being, or when we want to embrace something inspiring and moving that is outside of ourselves we unconsciously draw the curtain of our eyes. In both situations, there is a withdrawal of consciousness from the world. One is rejection and the other is acceptance. One is disturbing and the other is meditative. Whether we approve or disapprove, this response reflects from our being. And to make this response, whether it involves rejection or acceptance, we must journey to the core of our being. Our vision is unconsciously drawn inward because we wish to return to our inner home.

We want to ascend from our limited perception to unlimited experience. When our eyes are closed consciously, with the true purpose of experiencing the very essential self within us, we are in a state of fine-tuned meditation. We are reminded of our eternal existence and the infiniteness of our inner consciousness.

We keep the laws of our minds at bay while we are in a state of meditation, at one with ourselves. Great experiences happen. When we are not in a meditative state of consciousness, the laws of the mind eclipse us again. Then we start worrying, selfishly, about ourselves and the questions that arise are also mainly about ourselves. Such is the influence of the mind, which contradicts what we experienced moments before. This is the reason we have to be consistently, consciously aware of the truth, that life is a combination of discipline and love, rationality and emotion, logic and intuition, and physical perceptions and mystical experiences. We have to experience both, but we should dwell more on the side of love. The mind reflects discipline, and the heart reflects love. This will allow us to communicate with the world outside without losing our connection with the inner self.

Spirituality is a gracefully adventurous inner journey and a silent battle for balance between the logical mind and the loving heart.

Scientists often discuss the complexity of the human brain, its intricate functions and workings. However, there is another realm of research that has yet to be considered and this is the human heart, seated within, as the mother of the mind, the sense of the senses. The brain is physical, the mind is semi-physical (mystical) and the heart is spiritual. The heart, which eventually prevails, is purely a spiritual entity, and is addressed differently by people of different faiths and different schools of philosophy.

The world would not exist as it does, and creation would not have been challenging to us, if there had not been temptations, distractions and obstructions to hinder the flow of life. Because these types of resistance exist, it is of huge interest to consider how we can protect ourselves from negative forces and hindrances and how we can appreciate each moment of our lives, whilst moving towards a higher consciousness. When we talk of height, we tend to think of a vertical, physical height, because we are subject to the law of gravity. The experience we have of the physical laws in the world outside us, and our understanding of the concepts involved in these laws, change as we explore the deeper universe within us.

As we journey into the inner realms of our consciousness, using the consciousness manifested on the surface of our minds, using our will and our desire, and in silence, we begin to feel and experience the gradual change in the spectrum of the laws we recognize, away from those we accept with the intellectual mind. Our presence becomes vast and spacious and all artificial barriers and boundaries break away, inviting abundant peace and serenity into our being. When we reach the level of the heart, our personality is different from that which we had while dwelling in the mind. Our spirit becomes recharged and revived. *Now we are more than just an ordinary human being; we have become a special cosmic being.*

Although we believe that the laws of nature apply throughout the universe, their physical manifestation may be different, depending on where in the universe we are. If we go to any extreme, our experience of the universe changes. As we move away from the earth, the effects of the earth's gravitational field become weaker, and effectively we 'float' until we start to feel the effects of the gravitational field of another celestial body. The law of gravitation is the same everywhere, but the *effect* of gravity that we experience varies from region to region in space. Even on earth, gravity varies slightly from place to place. Similarly, laws and their effects vary as we journey into the inner realms of our consciousness. In this way our understanding deepens.

Those who live merely within the boundaries of the laws of the mind behave differently from those who have evolved spiritually. Thus, sometimes the behaviour and attitudes of a spiritual person may surprise and bring wonder to others.

One person may be intellectual, while another person is innocent. The innocent person can offer respect to the intellectual person as well as to another innocent person. However, one intellectual may barely show true respect to another because he or she finds it hard to accept the other as an equal. There is a conflict of ego. The person who is innocent is humble and simple but may be more resourceful in many respects. One cannot be both intellectual and humble or innocent without having spiritual awareness or undergoing spiritual awakening. Humility adds grace to the intelligent mind.

As we journey with our surface awareness from the mind to the heart, to our inner consciousness, we become profoundly aware of, and experience, our uniqueness.

II

FULFILMENT

Unconditional blossoming

3

Seeking Love and Searching for Truth

Truth cannot be experienced wholly, but it can be understood deeply. Love *can* be experienced profoundly in one's heart. Truth is like the father of all that exists, and love like the mother.

Searching for love means searching for the reflection of one's feelings and emotions in another person or in nature. It also means experiencing one's heart – that is, one's emotional and spiritual heart. This experience takes away one's sense of being alone, and makes one sensitive, creative, humble, open and intuitive. As one progresses on the inner journey, one attains an increased receptivity to nature and an enhanced ability to empathize. This leads one to feel love, which is a force of unity.

Searching for truth means searching for answers, clarity and true self-knowledge, reaching the core of understanding of one's self and one's connection with nature and the universe. The spiritual inner journey encompasses an external voyage to seek inspiration. When this journey is complete, it forms a circle that begins and ends in the spiritual heart. The return home is enriched with newly acquired impressions of information, energy and inspiration.

This journey is mystical. The wish expressed by many seekers, 'to experience truth', is not well phrased. Truth cannot be the whole of experience in the quest, but it is the discovery of truth within one's spiritual self that leads one to a discovery of truth in creation. The whole experience in one's quest should embrace the twin realities of the realization of truth and the feeling of love.

In the search for truth, one may be well read, but experiencing one's inner spirituality is more important than mere philosophizing. As the search for truth yields a 'rain' of answers, the flames of curiosity in the mind gradually become calmed and extinguished. In the course of reaching truth on that strenuous path, we tend to forget the heart.

If we do not exercise the truth of the self by thinking of good, by becoming good, by doing good and by letting the flower of self blossom in silence, then we become weak and ignorant of the treasures and spiritual abilities we possess within. For instance, every limb and organ in the body must be felt, sensed, remembered and exercised. If this does not happen, that particular part of the body will become atrophied. This may be tested. Suppose we do not wash or clean our faces for a week. We do not look at our faces in the mirror. We do not allow anyone to touch us, nor do we touch our faces ourselves, either with our hands or with anything else. If we photograph our faces and monitor the readings of our bodily functions and weight before starting this experiment and we take another photo after the week's experiment, we will see that the second photo is dull. It takes some time to regain the lustre and feel of the face. We cannot separate ourselves entirely from any part of the body, including our hair and nails. They need our conscious attention. They need our care, love and touch.

As the mind is somewhat different from the physical brain, the spiritual heart is not the same as the physical heart; it resides in and around the physical heart. The brain and the heart work together to facilitate the communicative network of blood, energy and nerve impulses. The mind and the spiritual heart have different effects and roles in our lives.

As we bring our focus down into the heart centre through gestures, or by touching the chest silently with our palms whilst wishing to experience pools of energy at the centre, we feel something uplifting and expanding. This positive experience occurs in minutes and, if we become more absorbed in experimenting, we achieve greater benefits. We may call this bliss or a state of joy – but these are simply names. What we intend or mean by the name is what matters. It is what we experience that counts.

Feeling is like water, emotion is like waves in the lake of consciousness.

As one progresses in this personal experience, one witnesses the evolution of one's being. Personality, voice, movements, attitudes and viewpoints noticeably change for the better. Some very rationally minded people can appear weak or emotionally dry. We sense this at the first meeting as we shake their hands, exchange greetings and begin to converse with them. Although they are good human beings, they seldom radiate peace because the power to transmit one's energies can be developed only through a spiritual approach. However, people who live with acceptance and simplicity reflect peace and pleasantness. Why do women normally live longer than men? One of the reasons is that they keep the emotional self alive and active, which helps the cells in the body live longer.

The search for truth has no final destination; it is a long voyage. The unconscious purpose of any seeker is to find inspiration, the true reflection of his or her being in some outside source. The source could be a person, or a place or even sometimes an object. After achieving this, the seeker returns to their heart with raised consciousness and enlightened awareness of their deeper spiritual self. A searcher will always return to the point of starting and is bound to meditate on all that they have undergone in the process of the quest, bringing the enlightening experience of purification. Most seekers searching literally for truth desist at some stage and realize in silence that truth is infinite and the human mind cannot comprehend it with absolute perfection. Eventually realization of higher knowledge takes place, accompanied by mystical and spiritual experiences – soaked in the tender love that is enlightenment. The very Self within us is part of the Universal Self. After this has been realized, the truth is recognized and embraced. Every human being has an innate tendency to search for truth. The circle of the journey and quest must be completed. The seeker has to return to their origin; otherwise realization of the purpose of the voyage cannot take place.

Seeking love means experiencing oneness and unity in our hearts, our consciousness and our being, with nature, with every being and with the universe. The heart is the destination, the mind is the voyager. The search for love is the grace-filled voyage into the inner realms of consciousness. In this search, one does not become tired or weary, but re-energized and creative.

Seeking love is not as complex as searching for truth. A simple yet profound experience of love takes one to the same height as does the search for truth. In the end, this search brings contentment.

4

Truth

In human consciousness, truth is a deeper and clearer understanding of the tangible world. Truth is a pure, logical, rational and philosophical means of comprehending the visible universe and the way it functions. In a much broader context, not only does truth provide a clear understanding of our own existence, as well as that of other species and of nature, but the realization of truth also comprises physical, mystical and spiritual experience.

Questions appear at the surface of the mind like bubbles floating on water. These questions can be loud and provocative. One subtle doubt or curiosity can give birth to myriad questions. When questions constantly arise in the mind, we have very little awareness of the answers hidden within. Answers do not fall like raindrops from the sky onto our heads.

The journey we embark on is circular. When we are seriously concerned about a particular topic or question, the same questions return to us again and again and eventually lead us to the required destination, where we find the answers and our fulfilment. The same human mind that gives birth to questions also has the innate ability either to find answers within or to search for answers outside. Clear answers emerge from our deeper Self when our quest for truth is single-mindedly pursued. An interrogative mind is always restless, as it constantly weaves loops of questions. Sometimes this leads us into a labyrinth of confusion. An inquisitive mind cannot stop asking questions.

When serious questions related to life, nature and the universe are approached from a scientific and rational angle alone, rather than being complemented by spiritual inquiries, the questioner may become entangled in a further surge of questions, resulting in even greater doubt and confusion. At this point the searcher has to struggle to find freedom. An intelligent person may look at the ignorant person, who seems to be in a state of bliss, but both are missing something: the intelligent person has the knowledge but not the bliss of ignorance or necessarily the bliss of innocence; the ignorant person does not have the awareness to recognize their state of bliss. Wanting to be in neither of these states alone, a seeker wants to achieve both the bliss of ignorance and the hiss of intelligence. If a seeker becomes discouraged and gives up the journey half way, they will have neither. This is when the seeker needs more inspiration, more endurance and determined persuasion, not based on aggression but on grace. Once the seeker attains the height of awareness and a certain state of enlightenment, then the enlightened seeker will have the rare ability to empathize with both the intelligent and the humble.

In the human brain, neurons are loaded with information in the form of chemical codes. A large proportion of our energy is absorbed or consumed by brain cells and, as a result, some people seem exhausted and perplexed. Whatever they do, the accumulated information cannot be released. They do not sleep well and have no real rest, which means even more work for their brain. Their dreams are also very complex. Their eyes flicker more during sleep; technically they have more rapid eye movements (REM). Their heart simply pulsates obeying the laws of physiology, but there is no learning from the experience and no deepened awareness. Their heart pumps blood mechanically, yet it suffers from bleakness or emotional aridity. Eventually they realize that simply understanding the physical aspects of life and seeking answers is not enough. One has to immerse one's being in meditative experiences, moving between silence, sound and melody. Outer nature is outside our body and mind, whereas inner nature is within us in a unique way that is largely undiscovered. Experience of both inner and outer natures can bring fulfilment and contentment in life, leading one to raised consciousness and deepened awareness.

Questions cannot arise without one being in possession of a seed of information. We have an ingrained urge to ask questions, to read books and listen to lectures. When we find them, some answers seem so familiar that often we feel we have already heard a particular answer from someone, somewhere. We have questions about life and we are searching for answers. Someone walks up to us and asks the question we have been asking ourselves. Then something awakens and inspires us intuitively and we give an answer to that person, which is very relevant to the question and the questioner's circumstances. From that day on, our original question about life disappears. A new question may arise, but the question that has been answered will not arise again. We are moved that the answer we sought for so long came from within ourselves. When questions are reflected back and resound within, this is spiritual inquiry. When the inquiry is serious and consistent, it leads us to experience new and different dimensions of our being.

When we find a source to reflect our being, the answer emerges like a lotus flower in the lake of the heart.

Our spiritual evolution makes us very special. We have the mystical ability to communicate by using our thoughts, through silence or sometimes just through the use of a few words. We enjoy the grace of our being and become inspiring examples. People who have sharpened their minds with the fire of rationality or mere intellectualization can explain much, but their explanations do not touch the heart because they have not spent enough time developing the inner experiences of their hearts and feeling the waves of emotion and the vibrations of their consciousness.

A newborn baby does not have a questioning tendency because the baby's mind has only just begun to develop in the brain, hence the baby is appealing and mystically attractive. The baby reflects only what comes from the heart and the high-magnitude life energies that surround it like an aura of light can be compared to the aura of suffused light we see around a full moon. If we spend a little time with a baby and observe carefully with patience, we experience love and innocence.

In the advanced stages of life we may return to our original pristine state of innocence and simplicity. There are only minor differences between a newborn baby and some persons of mature age, because both live at the level of the heart. The intellectual mind may gradually shrink to a simple mind and only those memories that are deeply imprinted on a person's consciousness remain. Mere knowledge does not bring total realization of the self; instead deeper, insightful experiences must accompany one's knowledge of the self.

Spirituality is a means of expanding one's consciousness by gaining wisdom through the practice of pure disciplinary logic and gaining deeper mystical and spiritual experience of the individual Self and of the connection between the individual Self and the universal Self. This process is an adventurous journey from the mind to the heart to consciousness. Self-realization is an experience that leads one through the various stages of the unfolding of one's true Self.

Truths can be compared to raw vegetables; they may be nutritious but on their own they do not constitute a delicious meal. However, when accompanied by spices and other ingredients, they can make a mouth-watering dish. Sometimes the expression of raw truth becomes necessary, but when that same truth is presented with art and heart, then it becomes a message that goes to the core of a person without causing any pain. Thus it creates a long-lasting and moving impression.

5

Truth and Love

By nature, truth is masculine, direct and unyielding unless pursued.
Love is soft, feminine and subtle.

Truth comprises knowledge and wisdom. It is the means by which we perceive and comprehend the universe, life and our consciousness. Truth is perceived from different angles and dimensions; hence it is not the same truth when we discuss it with others. We can imagine that truth comes in different colours or frequencies, like light waves. Some like the colour red, but others like violet or blue. Everyone has his or her own perception and taste. Thus, there are different religions in the world because each prophet, each holy person, comprehended the truth in their own mind, in their own way, or in the way in which they were inspired by higher nature. Therefore, each religion talks about the same truth, but the perspective, approach and presentation of truth are different.

Truth branches out in many directions, in the many flavours and colours of the frequencies of higher consciousness. From this assortment we choose what we want, whatever appeals to us, whatever suits our existence. Those who comprehend only the surface truths of life and the universe deny the truths that are perceived differently by others, thus creating conflict and

25

disharmony. Such people may become fanatics. Yet truth as an entity is not millions of miles away from us. It is within the sphere of our existence, consciousness and unconsciousness. Everyone has their own unique code with which to access it.

Love leads us to reach the true Self, from the mind to the heart to deeper consciousness, to the true Self within. Then the realization of truth dawns and connects us to truth outside our existence. This journey may take time, but it is possible.

Enlightenment attained from the pursuit of truth alone has its own merits, but it may not be encouraging and inspiring to budding seekers. Such enlightenment may be fulfilling to the enlightened, but it is a parched realization of truth without the dew of experiencing love in the heart. Attaining the height of consciousness in both the head and the heart brings greater fulfilment to the enlightened and to the seeker searching for guidance and inspiration.

Love cannot be understood intellectually because it is a deep experience. Truth, however, cannot be reached only through experience. We realize truth in many ways by questioning, rationalizing, analysing, experimenting and contemplating, from the most sensitive issues to major and complex matters. The volume of truth we are able to realize in our lifetime will be minute. We learn more only to know that we know very little or almost nothing at all, and we may become dissatisfied that our quest is not complete. Yet we do not give up, since life itself is a journey to reach higher and higher levels of consciousness. We should embrace both truth and love in our spiritual quest, to make our inner journey whole and cosmic with fulfilment and enlightenment; the remaining part is only celebration.

Buddha searched for truth for many years until he achieved enlightenment, but he emphasized compassion to humanity in his messages. In fact, whether we seek love or search for truth, we become compassionate and we blossom. Seekers may start in a search for truth but will end in the experience of love that leads them to enlightenment.

At the beginning of one's quest, truth is comprehended by one's clear mind with honest logic, whereas love is experienced from the heart. Truth brings clarity; love brings freedom. Searching for truth means searching for one's own truth within.

Love is experienced in one's heart. Love can unite everything into oneness. Truth cannot. Since the perception of truth is usually in the mind, whether we reach the truth or realize it, it is within the horizons of our consciousness that perception can differ between individuals or communities of different faiths and religions. Debate and conflict arise, which result in the setting of boundaries and the labelling of identities. This is inevitable until we discover the underlying spiritual truths individually and collectively.

Both love and truth are our metaphysical parents. Truth is the father, love is the mother. Love and truth pervade the world, the universe and all of humanity, whereas the perception of truth among individuals differs. When it is hard to find harmony and peace within the family on the basis of logically presented ideas and concepts, how can we harmonize our thoughts with others?

When we reach the highest point in our understanding and experience, either individually or collectively, we see ourselves and we see unity and oneness. With the expansion of consciousness, we see ourselves in everyone and everything, because of the experience of love. If there is no harmony within, love cannot be felt and the currents of love cannot flow. Empathy, harmony, compassion, kindness and forgiveness are all petals of the same flower of love.

In reality, wherever we start from, we end up at the centre, because truth is at the centre of everything we think of, everything we imagine. Eventually, we are led into the centre of truth in the circle of creation.

A newborn baby does not have any knowledge or understanding about healing him or herself. Yet that child can heal others. While the baby is among people suffering from painful ailments, some will be healed or their pain will be mitigated. This is the power of innocence.

We cannot experience peace when we reject something about ourselves or others. Peace begins to flourish in our minds and hearts when we start our day with acceptance, before we change ourselves or change others or find a solution to a problem. When we begin our endeavours with acceptance, peace ripples from our being. When we start to try and alter a circumstance or give advice to someone with rejection in our minds, then peace and harmony become distanced from us.

Truth and love are the twin realities of life. Through science and technology, we attempt to touch the hub of physical truth. Truth is nearest to our being and we should embrace it. Then, feelings of love flow like cascades of water. Truth is like a flower, and love is like the flower's fragrance – which spreads all around. In love, we experience freedom. In love we are prepared to give more than we receive. We feel the freedom of our spirit without conditions. We feel unrestricted and weightless. By saying less, we express more with our eyes, gestures and heart.

III

THE ESSENCE

The same essence but different containers

6

Religion and Spirituality

Religion is individual. Spirituality is universal.

Our inquisitive minds have driven us to explore earth and space. While exploring the earth, we came across other people of different races and faiths and communicated with them to achieve collective social and material expansion. With the growth of our awareness, of science, technology and industrialization, we began to travel to different regions. This helped religion to flourish on a global level.

In the past, spirituality was localized and marketed as a specific brand of religion. These religions were practised only by the community who lived in that specific region. Ingrained dogmatic views and ritualistic practices led to fanaticism among many such religions, and this hindered our understanding of the universality in our nature. Inevitably, this caused numerous battles under the banner of religion and truth. We built walls of self-centredness that warped communication because we had a blinkered vision of our lives and our relationship with nature. Each religion promised that the realization of truth was possible only by following the path that it prescribed.

Thus people with a common faith clustered together and cherished their religion. Religion became the central theme of everyday life and it gave birth to culture and politics. The influence of religion is so strong that politicians exploit religious beliefs even today. In the past, religious authorities controlled politics. Administration and policy-making differed from one religion to another. Beliefs, customs, clothing, eating habits and even medicinal systems were tentacles of religion. Long-cultivated habits, practices and traditions took on unique characteristics in people's psychology, as culture became the consort of religion. Even today, we have not completely forgotten our differences. Though we have made considerable progress in many spheres of life, we still witness religious conflict.

Ask any religious person about their beliefs and they will say, 'Our religion is the best,' or will imply that their faith alone can bring peace and the realization of truth. If this is true, why do multiple religions exist in the world? There should only be one. The question of religion can be phrased very simply: *At first we should believe in and practise humanity; only then will we be able to comprehend the essential truths of all religions, which are like pillars of universal truth.*

Though religions appear different on the surface, as we probe further we realize that we are all talking about the same ultimate understanding and absolute experience of the same universe.

When truth is comprehended with open minds and receptive hearts, we witness a panoramic effect in our lives. We can use the analogy of the rainbow. The sun's rays cause a rainbow when they are reflected by raindrops. We see the colours of the rainbow, even though the light comes from a single source. Similarly, human minds have moved closer and closer to

31

comprehending the ultimate truth, and that ray of ultimate truth has been subject to a rainbow effect, which is experienced as diverse religions. Thus *each religion reflects part of the spectrum of truth.* When we become open to the truth around us, we make a leap in the expansion of our consciousness and also have the opportunity to experience the different shades of truth. Only at that point does the spiritual journey become more effective and significant.

One's religion is like the relationship with one's real mother. That relationship does not stop one receiving motherly love from others and acknowledging a surrogate mother.

Those who do not imbibe the very essence of religion remain dogmatic and even fanatical, becoming addicted to mechanical rituals or religious acts. There are many religious people who have not read their own holy text, but who simply worship superficially. This is blind adoration, where emptiness prevails.

Love with knowledge and meaning cannot be affected by the passing years. Love without knowledge and meaning lacks the foundation to stand the test of time.

Religion is a package. Spirituality is its contents. If one remains only a religious person, one worships only the package. One adores the cover as an artefact, noticing only surface names and other historical details. Such people disregard other religions because of blind love for their own.

When a religious person is spiritually inspired, then they attempt to open the package and experience its spiritual contents. Then realization dawns. If the package were physical, one could use scissors or knives to open it easily, or one could read a manual on opening it without damaging the contents. However, the package of religion is abstract. One needs to undertake deep contemplation before one can understand and experience the contents; *only then* will universal understanding and collective spiritual enhancement become possible.

There is an ever-growing spiritual awareness in the world today because science has aided the investigation and understanding of the truths hidden in ancient practices and philosophies. It has also helped us to comprehend certain themes with greater trust and more receptive minds.

Since the subject of psychology emerged as one of the branches of academic study, human consciousness within the living brain has been taken seriously as a study. There was a time when consciousness by itself was ignored as being simply a superstitious element. Only in recent decades has human consciousness become a serious subject of study and research in its own right. As technology has advanced, it has helped us to probe into brain activity and to understand and study thought patterns. Now we can measure electrical and chemical activities in the brain, even when a person is in a state of unconsciousness.

What is self-awareness? It is knowing one's own self, not the self of another. Self-awareness does not end with theoretical knowledge of one's self, but incorporates in-depth experience of the many facets of one's being.

This is much like the example of students who are sitting in an examination hall. Although they sit together with an examiner or teacher supervising them, each student has to make her own effort to pass the exam. Though the students are sitting so close to each other, they cannot share their experience and knowledge because they must respond to their own question papers. Each has her own identification, and will receive her own grading after completing the examination. If one student passes, that is to her own credit. This credit cannot be shared with a student who has failed.

Each spirit is hosted in an individual physical body. *We have to make our own effort, in our own unique way, to attain knowledge and experience of the true Self.* The religion that we have followed is like a runway. At some point the seeker of truth must take off at the end of the runway and experience the flight of spirituality with freedom. This is the point at which fulfilment occurs.

Often inspiration comes from intuition that dwells in the heart and is the mother of intellect, and sometimes it comes from the heart of nature outside us. The whole process is a spiritual journey, a journey that begins with religion but does not end with it.

7

Experience and Illumination

Experiencing is spiritual. The instrument of experience is physical. The essence of experience is spiritual. By contrast, explanation, analysis, research, study and the body are all physical matters.

The experience of the world outside us becomes effective and profound when we have a focused mind, a sound body, alert senses and an incisive intellect. However, to experience the internal world, an alternative method is required: from sound to silence, from mind to heart, from thinking to feeling, from intellect to intuition, from the physical body to the non-physical self, from the egotistical mind to the humble heart.

We cannot remain totally inactive at any time, since our universe, which is the substratum of our existence, is functioning relentlessly, as is our body, with the mind existing as a by-product of body and consciousness. Hence, we are bound to think, feel, act and react. Most of the internal functions of the body are involuntary. When, however, we translate our thoughts, desires and wishes into actions by the use of our will, then that expression is a voluntary act. Our body acquires and expends energy constantly, but much more energy is spent when we engage ourselves in mental or physical voluntary action. Thinking means being awake and being awake means undertaking the process of thought. Sometimes thoughts occur involuntarily, although most of the time we contribute conscious energies to the world of our own thoughts. The expenditure of energy is inevitable as long as we exist. It is clear that, in order to expend energy, we have to have acquired it from some source. There is more energy loss in thinking than in merely engaging in physical action. There is increased energy loss when we deliberately engage ourselves with our thoughts for a long period of time. The activities of the mind can have tremendous energy consumption. At rest, the brain may utilize 20% of the total energy expenditure of the body. Medical studies have demonstrated that energy utilization of the brain is related to the number of nerve cells actively transmitting signals. Thus, as brain activity rises, there is increased oxygen consumption, which may be more than twice the normal expenditure in some areas of the brain. That is one of the reasons why most serious thinkers, who are mainly engaged in constant reading, writing or thinking, usually feel drained and exhausted. They have to compensate for this by eating and drinking more and having extra sleep; otherwise this tendency will have a negative impact on their bodies and minds. Usually such professionals or thinkers appear to have flickering eye movements. It means deep thinking consumes much glucose and burns more calories than physical work. In these individuals, their presence is predominantly felt in the head, since there is wilful disciplined expression of consciousness energies. This is the result of an emphasis on thinking, which is contrasted with deeper feelings.

Dhyana is spontaneous inspirational fine-tuned intuitive meditation, focused more on the level of the heart. During Dhyana, the sheer number of brain neuron cells that are active decreases. In fact, there is greater synchronization of the remaining active cells, which allows the seeker to be more focused. During the sleep state, there is a slowing of the brain waves, which can be seen in EEG (electroencephalograph) testing. Research shows that the alpha waves are indicative of deep sleep, which is most restful. During Dhyana, waking brain wave activity should similarly slow, corresponding to the change in neuronal activity. While conscious waking brain activity requires greater energy expenditure when focused outward, Dhyana does not drain the practitioner's energies; instead Dhyana brings peace, a feeling of oneness and renewed strength.

We cannot remain energetic and enthusiastic throughout the day. Our bodies and minds constantly urge us to reduce the amount of physical activity we are engaged in and to moderate the intensity of our thinking. Consider the analogy of going to work and coming home. When we go to work, we become consciously externalized; when we come home, we become internalized, loss of energy is minimized and we find peace, restfulness and relaxation. This is the dance of our existence, a dance of consciousness. When we become aware internally in a spiritual sense, we celebrate the dance.

When we deeply experience our being, sometimes in our minds and at other times in our hearts, we celebrate the dance of existence, the dance of consciousness.

When we are engaged externally, we exist more in the mind and less in the heart. During this period, a greater amount of energy is spent and we cannot remain in that state of expressiveness for a long time. The body becomes tired, the mind becomes weary and, as a consequence, our concentration weakens. We need rest, silence and refreshment to re-energize. We want to be ourselves. We need space. After this state of body, mind and consciousness has been achieved, a natural urge arises to socialize, to express what is within. This is a wave of consciousness, a wave of life, sound to silence and silence to sound.

Similarly, day and night, winter and summer, birth and death, creation and dissolution are all waves of energy, consciousness and nature. We feel more content and attuned to the universe when we have internalized the mind. When we do this consciously, we can release spiritual energies that can be spent in the world.

Condition the body, discipline the mind and free the heart. Let the spirit experience life.

Sound represents our physical existence and the visible universe; silence represents our spiritual existence and the invisible forces that sustain the visible cosmos. Silence is not simply the absence of sound but, as sound is an entity, so too is silence. It is an entity that can be captured with a sane mind and serene heart. Sound is physical; silence is spiritual. There is a stage between the waves of sound and silence that is mystical, where a melody that has universal appeal resonates. It makes the heart blossom and allows the mind to become tranquil. This melody heals the body and the mind. In order to experience the grace and harmony of life one has to experience and accept life with an open mind and a receptive heart.

When we are in silence, we become true to ourselves.

Rational inquiry, scientific research, creative emotion, intuitive awareness, mystical insights and spiritual experiences constitute a life of fullness. We cannot find absolute silence (stillness) in the world or in space, since the universe involves action. Sound is relentless and emanates constantly both internally and externally, but, despite complex physiological functions occurring in the body, we experience relative silence within. This is an amazing gift.

Once the spirit that operates the physical body disappears, the physical body becomes matter alone. Therefore, if we say, 'I love you,' who or what are we addressing? Is it the body? Is it the clothes that a person is wearing? Do we love the person's nature, or something else? It is evident that 'I' and 'you' are nothing but the individual, invisible, conscious entities, expressed in the physical.

Love is a connective force, an attractive, mystical force, a force of unity. The physical body is an instrument and a medium of communication. Love is always related to one's heart, not to one's mind, one's body or one's appearance. Hence there is no such expression as 'I love you with all my mind'. *That which truly experiences love is a deep-seated, conscious being within the physical body*, which uses many methods to gather new impressions of experience at every moment. For example, the eyes are used like a camera and the ears like a microphone. All the different experiences of physical existence are assimilated by this conscious being, resulting in a unified experience of all we are. This is the reason we create robots in the image of our own bodies. When we create, that creation is part of our nature.

First, we experience the world intuitively through our feelings. Then we unconsciously translate these feelings into definitive thoughts and, after that, into words and actions. We are the most highly evolved beings on this planet, with awareness of others, our surroundings and ourselves, but the very roots of our existence are not understood or experienced by everybody. Only a few become internally adventurous, reaching their deeper inner spiritual selves, realizing who they are and what they possess within.

Generally, we are preoccupied with questioning and becoming entangled in a net of intricate questions; we become exhausted, confused and pessimistic. In this confused state, even if someone provides an answer, we are unable to be attentive or receptive since we have programmed our minds only to pose questions. We should not let the questions multiply and confuse us. Instead, we should write them down and contemplate them whenever we have the time and space to do so. After a while we will find a clue to the answer; then we can verify it with further research through either study or discussion.

How do we learn things? Who is the teacher? How did we get our questioning mind? Who wrote the first book? Just as we materialized out of the universe, so questions, answers, thoughts and visions emerge from our being. We are more than we think we are. We have made dramatic progress in many subjects, but we have lost the way home. We will be able to realize all of our resources and potential if we deepen our consciousness through silence and meditation.

In the course of achieving something externally, our hearts are forgotten since we are mostly engaged in our minds.

A moment of experience is more powerful than a lifetime of words.

In order to experience the deep-seated, conscious life-force, we have to penetrate many layers of the mind. This is an adventurous undertaking and it is sometimes a challenging one. Our inner-conscious life-force gathers experiences through the physical body and these become converted into highly sensitive impressions. If these experiences happen rhythmically, we do not feel any loss or discomfort. If they occur rapidly or for prolonged periods, then our stress levels increase, which results in the impressions manifesting themselves in stiff necks, aching backs or headaches. As a consequence of overflowing and irregular impressions, the body becomes damaged.

We do so many things without being consciously aware of them, perhaps because of social pressure. In this state, our efforts are mechanical. Our bodies are involved, our minds are partially involved, but we are not wholly involved. Time is wasted. We neither gain knowledge nor do we gather true experience of that act or action. To live thus is to live on the surface. Years seem like months. Many people express the regret that they grew old quickly, that they did not know that real life would pass them by. There was little conscious deeper involvement in their actions.

The lesson to be learned from this is that the body needs stimulation. Only then does it remain active and revived. The brain has to be stimulated by information via recreation, whether it is serious or light-hearted. The eyes have to be stimulated by light; the ears have to be stimulated by sounds. The whole body needs stimuli from time to time; only then does it maintain its vitality and vigour. Similarly, in order to keep ourselves awake spiritually we need inspiration, the metaphysical stimulation of the inner, I-conscious self. This is a critical point. People seek inspiration. Some are in search of their own reflection, not the physical reflection that they see in the mirror, but the reflection of their invisible, mystical personality.

The mind is a question, the heart is the answer, the body is a physical reality and human consciousness is an experience.

Everything has two facets of existence. One is physical existence; the other is invisible existence. An invisible force is acting behind the visible universe. The invisible, inner-conscious life-force is a dynamic force in the physical body. If the health of that inner consciousness is maintained, then even in physical pain we retain grace and serenity, because we have realized our very nature and consciousness. We live to the fullest. Illumination of the spirit; in other words, self-realization is not thousands of miles away from us but is close by. It is the most heightened state of spiritual experience.

We focus much of our energy and consciousness on the world around us. We study the nature and behaviour of others but we ignore or forget to explore the nature of our own existence.

We work hard to gain success, wealth and the acquisition of material things, but we forget to give comfort and love to our own selves. To do the latter is not selfishness but self-*awareness*. With the rise of self-awareness we gain self-knowledge, self-experience and the realization of the wholeness of our being, which is a physical, mystical and spiritual experience. After gaining that state of consciousness, our understanding and experiencing of the world and its contents becomes clearer and deeper; serving others follows without inhibition or selfishness. With that heightened consciousness we are able to serve or assist others with more grace and conviction than before. Even if we do not help anyone in the physical sense, our presence can bring happiness, or a sense of revival of others' beliefs, which helps them grow.

Energy is always released, whether we are conscious or unconscious. The expenditure of energy is not always under our control, but it is possible to alter energy levels. It is possible to attune ourselves to others. This is a mystical art, not just a skill. It cannot be taught technically; rather, it has to be learned or practised of one's own accord. People who want spiritual growth or illumination of their inner being are really more adventurous than those who seek challenges in the outside world because the internal battle is fought alone. In the outside world others assist us, but on a spiritual journey we have to protect ourselves from our own minds and from the invisible negative elements that exist outside.

On the spiritual journey we are gentle warriors, with love as a shield and smile as a sword.

If someone wants to trouble others, they will often achieve their goal. The universal forces rarely seem to intervene to stop them. Similarly, the same forces involved in destructive causes also accompany those who have the strong conviction that they are doing something constructive, something positive for themselves and others. The same universe that helps people achieve negative objectives also helps those who are searching for spiritual illumination. The inspiration we draw into our being from outside sources, by listening to someone else, by reading a book or by watching the sun rise or set, helps us journey to the inner dimensions of our being. Without inspiration, it is difficult to overcome the obstacles that are present on this journey.

Some obstacles are visible. Others are invisible. Many traps lie in store for us if we are not careful to maintain a balance between needfulness and needlessness. Hence, one requires a spirit of adventure to reach one's inner consciousness.

What is spirituality? It is the mother of all kinds of knowledge, a subject that encompasses all that cannot be learned through rational inquiry or by scientific investigation alone. Spirituality is something that relates to one's own inner self or anything that is related to one's spirit of vibration and feeling. Our body remains purely physical but everything that we experience physically is also a spiritual experience, since spirit-consciousness in the human body is the true experiencer. However, our day-to-day experiences with our senses do not constitute a complete spiritual experience.

The vibration of our spirit is experienced in many forms, sometimes physical, sometimes psychological, sometimes psychic and sometimes mystical. This is the experience of the same spirit on different levels, in different patterns. Every subject or object becomes a source of reflection of the same inner spirit. We recognize or identify things or beings in the world mainly with our feelings and vibrations. This means that everything is experienced or expressed in terms of varied vibrations of the spirit, and the body and mind become the main tools to achieve this.

Although the beginning and end of every experience is spiritual, we categorize our consciousness into three states: the physical, mental and the spiritual. As well as having the spiritual ability within us to understand and experience our lives on a deeper level, we also have the ability to empathize with the lives of others. While intellectual understanding is unidimensional and cannot accommodate our feeling spirits, the feeling heart and spirits can embrace and accommodate all these possibilities. Feeling is spiritual, whereas thinking is semi-spiritual and semi-physical; the heart is spiritual and our spirits remain in spiritual dimensions.

No one would say that the mind is in the heart. The mind exists in the head. Emotions manifest themselves from the heart and spread throughout the body and mind, like ripples on a pond. The inner consciousness of a newborn child is largely focused in the region of the heart. As the child matures, the manifestation of inner consciousness becomes less prominent in the heart and more prominent in the head. This is how children gradually lose their pristine beauty and innocence with the growth of intellect.

We can withdraw our consciousness from the head to the heart region, without nullifying the presence of consciousness in the head. Thus, innocence is remembered and re-experienced. As we become old, we are once more destined for a state of innocence. At an advanced age people do not think destructively; they rarely have any intention to harm others. They reduce their physical activities; their requirements are reduced to a minimum. Greed, lust, deception and hatred rarely affect them. They love to play with children since they can relate to each other, despite the huge difference in age and appearance. This is why children enjoy playing both with other children and their grandparents. There is a synchronicity of hearts.

If that innocence is deliberately re-experienced in our hearts, in silence, without letting the egotistical mind influence

45

us, then that is a spiritual adventure. We experience grace and the tenderness of innocence within us and, at the same time, we also experience mature intellect. These are fused together in the brilliant lightning of self-realization.

The beauty of innocence becomes more obvious as people grow old. Youth recedes as we mature, but memories and impressions of youth, the wish to remain young and youthful in spirit remain throughout our life. In the natural process of ageing we begin to discover and re-experience youthfulness in our hearts. A beauty that is enchantingly mystical unfolds. We become reminded of our innocence, and experience a sense of peace, in the presence of those who are closer to completing the journey of life, just as we find peace and beauty in the presence of the newborn.

All humans at the latter stage of their life journey back towards innocence and humility with a tender mind returning to a pure heart. Thus, they gracefully conclude the circle of life.

IV

WAVE OF LIFE

Silence deep within
Sounds on the surface

8

The Smile, a Gesture of Humanity

A smile is the reflection of one's blossoming heart.

A smile can alleviate pain, difficulty and discomfort, and may also have the power to heal not only the body, but a dejected mind or a heavy heart. A genuine smile is twofold in its positive effect, bathing both the giver and the receiver in a metaphysical sensation that is comforting and soothing. Smiling is a gesture that no one shuns. It elevates our energy levels, eases tension and creates a friendly atmosphere, conducive to dialogue between strangers. Even a forced smile generates positive vibrations – a fact often observed in business surroundings. A smile is a natural greeting of friendship and hospitality; it is warm and inviting, whether one is rich or poor, an academic or a layperson; a smile poses no barrier to communication.

It is ordinary to smile when one is content, but to be able to smile in times of difficulty is the mark of a very special person. A smile is inspirational. If someone really smiles at us from the heart, our heart treasures the impression of the smile for a long time, even though the mind may forget. The smile may be replayed and recreated in our consciousness, and we relive the joy and elation as if it were happening anew.

While laughter may be misunderstood, an ingenuous smile will not be misconstrued. Laughter can be social, but a smile means much more – it bears spiritual significance. Nature conferred this precious gift on humans, the only species on earth blessed with the innate ability to smile expressively, even though animals also have unique ways of expressing joy. Nature's precious gift, the ability to smile, is seen less and less in today's world. We should cherish this gift and not forget this natural ornament.

Some people attach conditions to their smile, and may smile when negative conditions disappear. But, if we wait for all our expectations to be fulfilled before we smile, then smiling may become alien to us. We all want to be positive, but often we become negative. It is because our increasing expectations and desires are not realized that we become pessimistic and emit such energy. It is then that philosophical understanding and spiritual contemplation can help us to overcome the obstructions that inhibit us from expanding our consciousness and experiencing the bliss and beauty of life.

The universe is multidimensional

There are infinite varieties of beings and celestial bodies in the cosmos. Because of this, our individual views are also different. Everyone has their own unique way of observing and absorbing the essence and meaning of the universe. The universe provides us with abundant choices, so we need not attribute everything to destiny. We have the freedom to choose. Many believe that the destiny of a person is predetermined. In truth, we determine our destinies by dint of our own individual nature, demeanour and character. For some, creation is an accident, a mere coincidence.

For others, creation is orderly, and therefore can be attributed to a creator. For some, there is no definite meaning to life; it is what one makes of it. For others, nature is wrought with meaning. They see love, beauty and unity in everything, though the ways of seeing are diverse. For a few, creation is disciplined and mathematical. For others, it is magical and mystical. For some, it is logical and philosophical; yet to others, it is a spiritual experience. We all see different dimensions of the same universe.

The universe accommodates every kind of thinker and believer. There is little to debate, everyone is simply talking about their personal universes in the common universe, according to their dimension of existence and personal experiences.

We can tune in with anyone or any situation, and experience life. For instance, if we tune in to see mainly humour in the world, then we will be laughing at every incident in life. Alternatively, if we tune in to believing and perceiving that the world is full of misery, then our thoughts will reflect this and we will experience life as miserable. Though we exist in a happy environment, our senses will resonate with unhappy images.

Some see themselves as students, and they learn lessons from every circumstance, every day. For some there is no creator, and reality has no deeper, hidden meaning. For others, everything is immensely meaningful and full of messages and truths; nothing happens by chance and everything happens for a reason, according to the will of higher nature. One can experience meaning in life and become sceptical about others' views and perceptions. For those who view or perceive the universe from a mystical angle, everything is mystical – the reflection in water, the reflection in mirrors, twinkling stars, the earth's orbit – from the way we exist to the way we perceive. The way all beings exist and interact, the effect of night and day, seasons, eclipses, and the way the human mind operates — all are mystical.

For artists, everything is artistic. The physical body is artistic. The way butterfly wings are designed is aesthetically superb. The appearance of a tiger, the feathers of a peacock with their perfect geometry and radiant tones of colour, are all the result of deliberate design.

When we observe the universe with conscious awareness, we find so much meaning in every moment. From the vibration of elementary particles to the arrangement of the Milky Way — one sees meaning everywhere. There is meaning in both pain and pleasure. Sometimes there is more meaning in pain than in pleasure, but it is a human tendency to turn to pessimism when encountering failure or painful situations.

Nothing is wasted in the universe; everything is recycled. Everything is transference and transmission of energy: expenditure of energy by one source and acquisition by another take place regardless of the nature of the activity involved.

Although our lifespan is shorter than that of some trees and animals, we are gifted with awareness. We are aware not only of ourselves, but also of others and of everything that surrounds us. We have the ability to raise our awareness and consciousness and to recognize ourselves as thinking beings. We are able to accelerate our growth both internally and externally.

9

The Ebb and Flow of Consciousness

On the cosmic scale, the physical form of existence is only a twinkling moment in the emergence of our spirit-being. We have merely taken shelter in a material body on this eternal journey through the cosmos.

Life's meaning

Early man and woman believed mainly in spirits. Whenever an incident occurred, they would pray. They believed that higher spirits controlled human spirits and that spirits controlled the universe and the forces of nature. If it did not rain, people prayed. If there was any danger, people prayed. They imagined that there were specific deities ruling specific elements in nature, particular diseases and human destiny. These beliefs helped our ancestors to survive and develop their spiritual abilities and to evolve gradually towards rationalization, intellectualization and enlightenment. The traces of these early beliefs can still be found today amongst people of the East, who believe that *first we are spiritual beings, then we are physical beings.*

Our spirits acquire energy from nature through our bodies and send energy in exchange, while retaining the impressions of these vibrational experiences in our bodies and minds. In essence, *life is nothing but a spiritual experience.* Some people are aware of this fact but many are not. By becoming aware that we are spirits vibrating our will through the body with the effect of consciousness, our experiences become much deeper and more concentrated. With this awareness we experience oneness via energies, thoughts, words and presence and we realize that life is long. There is a saying, 'Life is short and sweet' but, with this realization, the saying should be changed to, 'Life is long; make it a celebration'.

Life is short for those who merely skim its surface and engage in superficial activities. Most of the time they are not fully present in the moment, in whatever they are doing. As we learn to live in the core of our being, feeling the depth of words, actions and their consequences, we develop higher sensitivity. We can empathize with the feelings of others and we can communicate with nature and the forces of the universe. The universe is not dictatorial. Rather, it has all the time, space and compassion to listen to us. We have to rise above our limits by raising our consciousness. *Everything* is a spiritual experience, our thinking, speech, actions and the way we live. We are all spiritual beings. We become aware that we are spirits with consciousness *and* with a physical body.

There is a vast difference between speaking from the mind and expressing from the heart. When we express something with the sole purpose of impressing others, that expression may be impressive but short lived. When the same expression is created without an ulterior motive, then that expression is natural and inspirational, leaving a long-lasting positive effect on the minds and hearts of people. It may not always be practical from a worldly point of view, but it is possible to put our hearts into whatever we are doing in order that we can experience our consciousness, our presence and the way energies are received, transformed and transmitted. As a result life feels long rather than short because we are feeling the depth every moment far more than it appears on the surface.

Success and failure

Success and failure are interpreted relatively, but in actuality we are always successful if we live life at the level of the Heart. We never experience failure in the truest sense. From a philosophical point of view we are never lost; we are always somewhere, in touch with the deeper self. Failure encountered in the worldly sense, even after our best efforts, is a sign or gesture wrought with messages and guidance from the universe that are specially designed to suit our individual progress. If events unfold according to our expectations, we believe we are successful, but the truth is that the law of nature will not allow us to predict or dictate the outcome of each undertaking or every event. While every success is preceded by a proportionate fear of failure and risk, a dedicated, sincere endeavour is in itself a reward and gives rise to a feeling of satisfaction that you did your best in the circumstances. The outcome is however you interpret it to be. Some people are successful but they still regret that they did not achieve more. There is no end to endeavour since the learning process is always new. Regardless of our age, we are always young when we are learning.

There are definite reasons why not all actions bear fruit and we must delve deeper to learn why this is so.

When we develop trust in nature, our bodies and minds become capable of acting as conduits. We are able to realize our potential and our innate ability by gaining deeper insights as to our origin and true nature.

When we express our existence with high energy, enthusiasm and courage, and achieve success or victory in the material world, we experience more of the spirit in the body. When we become absorbed internally in silence and we find a different tone of experience, the body is a guest and the spirit is a host. This is mystical and very uplifting. This is a step beyond the previous state of experience. Although the effects are different in these two states of consciousness, a feeling of unity and oneness remains common to both. During the experience of the spirit in the physical body, we do not see much beyond the body-concept. In the experience of the body in the spirit, our attitude and views shift from the ordinary to the extraordinary.

When we believe that we are wholly responsible for everything that happens in life, we carry a great burden of guilt in our hearts. If we make a leap from this ordinary understanding to a higher understanding, then we realize that we can only do so much, though we do it with sincerity and good intention. Once our duties are performed to the best of our beliefs and capability, we become qualified to submit ourselves to a higher will where we experience grace, boundless energy and a sense of freedom. When we submit our egos to the universe, we become relieved of the iron-like hat of the ego. We rest at ease and in comfort.

Submission and progression

In submitting ourselves to higher nature, we are able to access the intuitive wisdom within. We free ourselves from artificial constrictions.

When we have submitted to nature in humility, we become attuned to the rhythm of the world and the universe, the rhythm of everything that happens around us. This is because spirit naturally tunes itself to the rhythm of nature. In this state we learn that we are not solely responsible for our lives. There are a myriad factors and forces that affect our lives, beyond our perception and understanding.

When we emphasize the physical experience of the spirit, we become one with the physical body because we descend into every layer of the being. Every physical move we make is a movement of the inner spirit, but in this state of consciousness these movements are well disciplined. We gain many physical, but few spiritual benefits. We gain the experience of the spirit, but unconsciously. Some people believe only in humanism or pragmatism. They do not wish to be recognized as seekers, although they move in a spiritual direction. By following humanity, being conscious of their duties, not intentionally hurting anyone and being helpful to others, they have already laid the foundation for their spiritual evolution, but may not be consciously aware of having done so.

The balance or alternative between the disciplined mind and the emotional heart is the mystical approach, which imparts knowledge and inspires us to gain deeper insights into the inner realms of spiritual truth. One cannot be spiritual without allowing oneself to be bathed in different kinds of emotion. Surging emotions have a cleansing effect on the unpleasant impressions stored in the deeper mind.

Over a great span of time, human consciousness makes a shift that is progressive or regressive, depending on our interpretation. In this process, nothing remains constant or stagnant. Everything moves in waves, in a pattern of high and low tides, ebb and flow. Such is the journey and the evolution of life, spirit, nature and the universe.

10

Potential

The desire to deepen our awareness, to know the true Self and to explore the full potential of our consciousness, is evidence of a profound truth; we are not limited human beings, we have a great role to play in the universe.

The parallel approach

While our imagination soars far beyond mind, body, time and space, the physical body is like an organic atom in the ocean of life. We often take it for granted and rarely appreciate what we have. We crave something that is beyond our reach, often far in the distance. There is an overpowering desire to be ubiquitous, but the laws of physics and the laws of nature do not permit us to achieve this in a physical sense. We can understand the laws of nature but we cannot go against them. Our bodies are fragile and vulnerable. Natural phenomena such as sleep, hunger, ageing and death cannot be absolutely overcome. It is possible to resist or delay their effects temporarily by using our vast stores of knowledge, our technology and our ability to work within nature, but ultimately, the physical body is finite. Here is a beautiful, mystical, cosmic paradox: in our finite bodies, we each have a unique and infinite spirit.

In truth, each of us knows deeply that he or she is an invisible, infinite spirit, sustaining and operating the limited physical body. The mind is a bridge between the physical body and the invisible spirit.

Consciousness means, in the normal sense, awareness of oneself, of others, of nature and of one's surroundings. In the evolution of all beings, especially humans, consciousness developed predominantly in the head region, a manifestation that we recognize as the mind. *The mind is but a by-product of our consciousness. The mind is not the whole of consciousness as is usually believed in psychology; consciousness is much deeper than the surface-manifested faculty we call the mind. For example, a mother can empathize with a child, whereas a child cannot understand what it is to be an adult.* This deeper consciousness motivates the mind towards understanding the physical truth of the universe through experiment, study, research and discussion. This process of exploring that particular dimension is how we have come to understand science and to develop technology.

The Self beneath our minds and hearts intuitively impels us to search for truth, love, meaning and the deeper experiences of life, a learning experience, a study of what is referred to as metaphysics, hyperphysics or spirituality. Thoughts and feelings exist as parallels – science and spirituality, mind and heart, logic and emotion. We try to embrace creation with parallel approaches to life. One approach brings us pleasure, excitement, entertainment, knowledge and comfort. The other leads us to profound spiritual experiences that add more meaning to our lives, resulting in contentment, peace, realization and enlightenment.

Over the course of time, we continue to adapt ourselves to different ways of understanding and experiencing our most essential being, the true Self. Some schools of thought developed into religions and some have become exclusively specialized so that they understand and experience one particular flavour of truth. However, all schools of thought have had one common aim, which was to find fulfilment in life. However, as we have advanced intellectually and intuitively through the evolution of human consciousness, we have become increasingly global. We embrace all that is possible in human life.

It is our innate desire to be adventurous and explore both our internal and external worlds. Our curiosity to journey, touch and experience the outer world does not stop upon reaching our intended goals and targets. However, it is the next step of embarking on an *inner* voyage with the objective for each of us of discovering the true Self that brings fulfilment.

There are two possible approaches to exploring our inner and outer universes. The curiosity we harness in approaching disciplined forms of study is straightforward, logical and direct; this is the method applied to learning within school and university. The alternative approach is the one we apply to experiencing the non-physical part of our existence. The first draws abundant energy from us but returns little, while the latter uses little energy but provides us with abundant peace, inspiration, insight and intuitive wisdom. The advantages derived from this spiritual approach also result in physical benefits.

With this alternative route to discovering the true Self and the treasures lying beneath the inner sea bed of consciousness, it is necessary to observe mystic silence and to redirect energies and resources from the mind to the heart in preparation for the voyage. Those who are determined to explore the inner side of their existence search for inspiration and seek out spiritual guidance or books to provide insight. *They search for truth.* It is through this inward journey, from the surface consciousness to the core of our inner consciousness, that we enjoy so many mystical and spiritual experiences. Each time we re-acquaint ourselves with our inner nature, we become increasingly connected to nature outside ourselves.

Over the last century, people have become more aware of raising consciousness, of the welfare of others, and of our earth's physical health, beauty and spiritual well-being. Beyond this, we have also started to explore the possibility of life elsewhere in the universe.

The desire to deepen our awareness, to know the true Self and to experience various states of consciousness are all signs of the truth, which is that we are not limited physical beings but infinite spiritual beings who have a great role to play in the universe. There is an invitation, outside of time, for us to explore the inner universe; the outward physical journey alone is not enough.

The physical journey in the outer world is symbolic, and reminds us that we should also journey into the mystical dimensions of our consciousness. There we will acquire the knowledge, awareness, intuition and guidance to embrace the beauty of creation with our hearts and spirits.

11

Living

There are three planes of conscious living: living in the mind, living in the heart and living in the core being.

There are primarily three planes of conscious living:

- Living in the mind. This is living a life of sheer materialism, living only by the application of logic. Everything is reduced only to the physical; nothing exists beyond that.

- Living in the heart or living with depth, with emotions, with feelings, with creativity. The heart is using the mind as an instrument to express its guidance – in emotional form, like poetry. The mind is used automatically but consciousness manifests itself mainly at the level of the heart.

- Living in the core being. This means living where consciousness has manifested itself predominantly in the deeper self, where your perceptions are beyond ordinary thinking. You can connect with people easily because the ability to empathize is very high. The self uses both the heart and the mind, the heart first and the mind next. This is living in the self, living in *Atman*. It is difficult to maintain this state of consciousness constantly.

There is a plane of consciousness that embraces all the above.

Human life begins in the core being. Hence, newborn babies live in their core being. During this stage of human development, young children possess tremendous energy, which has a positive influence. The presence of a baby in close proximity to a sick person tends to have a curative effect. As babies grow, their spirits move closer to the surface, which is the head region.

We describe the effect of spirit and consciousness in the head region as the thinking entity known as the 'mind'. The journey from core consciousness to the heart to the mind is a natural one. It is akin to setting out on a trip from one's home to the outskirts of one's province or country. The purpose of the excursion is for entertainment or to learn something, or to gain new experiences and return home safely with the impressions of our experiences and an expanded state of consciousness.

During adulthood, there is even less of a person's presence in the heart, and more of his or her presence in the head. We are more curious about the outside world than about ourselves. Our energy and resources are spent on learning and understanding the outside world through the mind and through the senses. As information enters our neural library through the cerebral cortex, we are affected by it. These effects will continue until we master the art of withdrawing our prevailing consciousness from the head to the heart, in order to protect ourselves against negative influences from the world and to prevent an excessive loss of outgoing energy. The more information that enters our brain, the more curious we become, and the more questions arise. As a consequence our inner space contracts, causing us to feel suffocated, restless or irritable.

There is no end to the mind's curiosity. The more information we acquire, the less we feel our presence in our hearts. This does not mean we should give up learning. We should continue to learn with ease, comfort and grace, but with awareness.

To live in the mind is to focus on one's inflexible ego, which leads to suffocation within. The ego is the nucleus of one's personality; we need the ego to maintain our individuality. A controlled ego can raise one's confidence and generate respect from others, while an uncontrolled ego renders us foreign to ourselves. After regaining control, we find it difficult to recognize ourselves in the actions we carried out under the influence of the exaggerated ego. Such is the negative effect of the ego. It can block our communication with people and it can stunt our personal growth.

We have to temper our egos with spiritual awareness and with the cooling fire of love from the heart. However, it is not healthy to become absolutely devoid of ego. A person who lives in the heart does have an ego, but that ego is like a coconut tree on an island. It can bend but it is strong. It bends when there is a hurricane or a storm, but as a defence mechanism and not as a source of conflict. Its shape, structure and beauty are restored after the incident. One cannot live without ego, but a flexible and tender ego allows for growth and also helps us find peace, comfort and reflection.

If we live solely in the mind, we lose our humanity.

The mind is more rational and less emotional, whereas in the heart there are waves of emotion but little logic. Logic cannot encompass all facets of life; it is only part of life. Curiosity, followed by common sense, logic and rationality, are orderly steps towards understanding the world and they lead us to an advanced awareness of physical truth.

Our technological achievements are primarily based on the logic of the mind and are the natural outcome of disciplining nature; examples include advances made in aviation and in computing. This does not, however, mean that miracles, human mystical experiences and invisible forces of nature no longer exist. They occur even more often nowadays but we choose not to recognize them.

Miracles and mysteries are exceptional incidents or events in nature. From individual lives to global awareness, there are many incidents that cannot be logically explained or analysed: the truth is that mysteries continue to exist. Even after thousands of years, miracles still take place.

Suppose one signs a business contract. There are many sentences explaining the terms and conditions of the contract, yet many unforeseeable occurrences may exist beyond its framework. For every new occurrence, new legislation is created. Some may be revised or revoked, but many new pieces of legislation are enacted to account for exceptions to existing rules. No matter how far-seeing one is, there are always unexpected incidents that must be accommodated.

If one is truly knowledgeable and sensible, one does not engage in the facile rejection of the statements of others simply because logic deems otherwise. Logic has a finite frame and a foundation of discipline, but our imaginations can soar far above the limiting frontiers of the intellect.

When we are at work, we behave in a particular manner. When we come home, we behave differently. In the workplace our behaviour is disciplined, because there we struggle for collective achievement. When we are at home, we are free of socially constructed attitudes and control. Similarly, when we return from an extended state of consciousness to the root of consciousness, we re-experience the exactness of the mind, the fullness of the heart and the closeness of being in the body and in innocence. After we return to the mind, we become aware of many changes within us. Our friends and families also notice something special unfolding within us. We see something beyond what we usually see in the world, since our perception has broadened and our intuition has become active. Above all, we have a clear vision of our existence and of the universe that is connected to us.

Nature has provided all the necessary resources to every being, proportionate to each person's level of consciousness and dimension of existence. The rest is left for us to explore, experience and express, thus honouring nature, the universe and creation. Above all, the same forces that created us also provide inspiration: meeting someone, watching and observing the different effects of nature, solitude, being with people, being in silence – all these can be sources of inspiration. We need inspiration to remind us of our home.

The return of consciousness from the mind to the heart is a mystical journey that contrasts with the physical journey we undertake in the world. It is more interesting and beautiful compared to an adventure in the outer world. External achievement, satiation of the senses or gratification of the mind cannot bring absolute satisfaction, but the inner voyage brings many positive changes, through which we are able to recognize, acknowledge and experience the world.

In the material world, growth means reaching higher ground. We use escalators to go from the ground floor to higher floors. Because of the profound influence of gravity on our minds and bodies, we think that progress means drawing a line from the bottom to the top; the same concept is utilized when charting graphs. But the spiritual journey, or spiritual growth, is the opposite of what we see in the physical world. We descend or move inwards, yet we are progressing. There are so many flashes in between, so many glimmers. Each person gains his or her own unique spiritual experiences, which are distinct from the experiences of others.

As we bring our conscious awareness, through an act of will, down from the central nervous system towards the heart centre, we experience many dimensions of our beings. These include experience of the mind, the heart, the deeper consciousness, the spiritual Self and many other facets previously unknown to us. Some experiences are physical, while others are emotional or mystical. Intuition blossoms as a flower blossoms. From infancy to adulthood, we are in a constant process of growth.

Since there is a strong, inseparable connection between human existence, human consciousness and consciousness in the cosmos, the whole living body is like a fruit of nature. If we study a fruit, we can extrapolate its root source, its region of origin and the conditions of its planting or harvesting. Similarly the fruit of the physical body with a conscious spirit within has the potential to understand, experience and connect with its source in the cosmos.

12

Life-Force

The living body responds when it is stimulated. Conversely, if there is no life, the body cannot respond to stimuli. The body alone does not have the ability to react to stimuli without the collation and co-ordination of the life-force within. Although a person may be in a state of unconsciousness, when a limb is forcefully stimulated by an instrument, the body reacts. Often, the response may only be measured by sophisticated cardiopulmonary monitoring, or by EEG recordings made of brain-wave activity. Yet current medical technology cannot measure all the functions and activities of the human body and, in extreme cases, this response may be delayed or may not even occur. Generally speaking, however, some response will take place because the life-force is present despite the person's lack of awareness of it.

The life-force is like fire and the manifestation of consciousness from the life-force is like heat.

In a wider context, everything is consciousness and consciousness is everything. Neither non-physical conscious life-forces, nor energy, nor the physical body alone can sum up the totality of a living entity that thinks, imagines, perceives and understands. Fragrance and flower, honey and sweetness, meaning and words cannot exist independently. When a person is in a state of unconsciousness, the life-force within the body becomes more conscious of itself. This keeps the body functioning with exquisite regulation of both the respiratory and cardiovascular systems. During that period, the life-force cannot respond immediately to outside stimuli because it has gone beneath the mind, deeper into the metaphysical heart.

Whether the physical body sustains the life-force or whether the life-force sustains the physical body is a mystery. For example, if you take a receptacle and pour some liquid into it, the receptacle will hold the liquid; the liquid does not hold the receptacle. However, the contents of the receptacle are just as important as the container. The receptacle of the body is far superior, magical even, compared with the ordinary containers we use in our daily lives. Receptacles normally do not interact with their contents, but this nature-made body receptacle can respond, think, feel and grow with the grace of the life-force in itself.

The life-force has four facets: time, which is made up of the past, the present and the future; the conscious (the life-force manifested on the surface in the head and in the mind); the subconscious (the same manifested in the deeper mind, conceptually at the throat region); and the unconscious (which is spread throughout the body from the very DNA molecules to bones, muscles, tissues and skin). The life-force assumes the outline of the body. The life-force has all the feeling and capacity to decide, control and operate an individual's destiny.

When one is in a state of unconsciousness, the life-force recedes from the outline of the body and curls into a sphere. During that time, a person becomes totally unaware of his or her existence, thus the life-force cannot immediately respond to stimuli. It has withdrawn from the head. In other words, the mind becomes absent from the head since the life-force, curled in on itself, is now more prominent at a deeper level. It tries to repair the body while at the same time holding the body or keeping it protected to the highest degree. It remains obedient to the disciplinary rules of nature; those of physiology, physics and gravity. Then the life-force resumes its original state, its true form of existence. It must become one with the body in the full sense and again takes its shape, its full outline. If someone were to move a hand over your body without touching it, you would be able to sense it. That means that the life-force is intense, its presence being felt all over the body.

As we choose to journey deeper into our being, we become more aware of our core consciousness and our whole being. We expand. With experiences at different levels at different times, we discover our presence and being, which is more than our mere physical existence.

We find ourselves in others and we find our reflection in the universe. Whoever comes in contact with us, we embrace them with more than our limbs. We are magnetic. We are elevated beings. We see others not only with our physical eyes, but also with our active, intuitive eyes. We hear the thoughts of others, even though they are silent. They feel unified with our energy fields and consciousness, though they do not know what they are experiencing. They feel happy to be around us without our making any effort. Even from a distance others feel our love and presence. With the growth of inner spirituality and with the expansion of consciousness, we are able to affect people positively. Though we may be unaware of the power of the life-force, its role and effectiveness are obvious.

V

LIGHT AND ENERGY

Combining the light of wisdom with youthful energy, an
adventure of balance

13

Darkness and Light

There is more darkness than light in the cosmos. At night, when we look up at the sky, there is intense darkness as far as the eye can see. Only here and there can we see stars twinkling. Such is nature's mystery. Yet light establishes its brilliance. Light makes its own way, penetrating indefinitely as long as it does not encounter any object or it is not scattered, for example by interstellar dust.

The sun is the antithesis of darkness. It is full of light and fire. Darkness gradually fades as the sun emerges and returns as the sun disappears gracefully in the west, to reappear on the other side of the earth. How perfect the universe is. It operates with the utmost precision and has reasons and meanings of its own.

Our logical minds are constrained by our physical bodies. Our minds think unidirectionally. In contrast, our free, non-logical hearts can visualize, feel and experience multidirectionally with extra intuitive ability. Many meditate facing the direction of light, enabling the body and mind to harmonize with electrostatic forces.

Darkness and light maintain their nature, properties and individuality in nature and throughout creation.

Our existence is not made up purely of light, meaning goodness, as many religious people believe. If our existence were made up of nothing but light then we could never even imagine darkness. We would never encounter negativity. We would always dwell in truth and love. The truth is, however, that our inner spirit represents light, whereas the body represents the opposite of light. Each complements the other. Hence, once the conscious life-force is no longer represented in the physical, then the body is no longer vibrant and attractive.

The inner spirit represents light, whereas the body represents the opposite.

As long as the body is illuminated by the spirit, the negativity of the physical body remains subdued and the body radiates life in each and every successive moment. While people who dwell more on the physical side become destructive, those who live more on the spiritual side become instruments of peace, love, inspiration and wisdom. Hence negativity resides within us rather than outside. We all have to struggle if we wish to be close to light and close to the very truths of the universe and creation. Only a spiritual approach and dedication can help us move in that direction.

The mind exists between the positive spirit and the negative body. We are easily influenced by untruths. In meditation, we are alone. In that state everything becomes clear. We do not experience doubt, fear or confusion. At some point we become aware of those words, thoughts and deeds that were wrong. We experience regret and realization. But, even after that realization and self-awareness, we again succumb to negative actions or thoughts and an onslaught of darkness. Only those who are spiritually inspired, those who are awakened or who have realized the inner light of truth will maintain long-lasting compassion, tranquillity and innocence in their hearts.

Many believe and worship light as the whole truth or light as absolute life. They expect life to go on smoothly without hitch or hindrance. They become idealistic and fantasize. With the purpose of getting closer to truth they move far away from the truths of existence. In their beliefs and philosophies they have failed to accept that darkness has an important role to play, sometimes a more important one than light.

According to research in physics, ninety per cent of the total mass of typical galaxies consists of dark matter that is known as galactic dark matter (GDM). Dark matter possesses an abundance of energy. For instance, a black hole (a star that has run out of its nuclear fuel) does not even let light escape from its gravity. Such is its power. Physicists have established that there is more dense dark matter in outer space than light. When we accept and experience both light and darkness simply as different expressions of the same creative forces of the cosmos, we begin to experience harmony within. Our physical bodies represent darkness and our inner spirits represent light. The truth is that the two have been combined mystically and gracefully into our lives. Hence the drama of life is intriguing as these opposites interact and react within our bodies and spirits, and also outside in the immediate external world and the grander universe.

14

Energy and Timelessness

The whole cosmos is nothing but energy. Everything we are aware of can eventually be reduced to energy.

All objects are time-bound. Although space seems to be interwoven with time, space is also independent of time. Space contains time. Which makes us transit from physics to metaphysics. The higher consciousness, cosmic consciousness, is timeless. The whole cosmos is nothing but energy. From elementary particles to giant galaxies and clusters, there is nothing that cannot be reduced to the flow and circulation of energy in different patterns and proportions. Only forms and shapes of matter change, being time-bound, whereas the core nature of energy remains unchanged locally, regionally and relatively; each quantum of energy varies but the sum total of energy remains the same in the cosmos as a whole. The core energy of every entity in the cosmos is the same throughout creation and this will be proved as we advance in understanding the core of our existence.

Where energy does manifest differences is in its functions and processes, such as kinetic energy, potential energy, mechanical energy, chemical energy, electrical energy. These energies vary in their patterns of activity and in their effects on a body or on a concentration of matter. The relative distribution of energy varies in time because of the process of change that is operative in action and reaction. However, the sum of the total energies of the universe will always remain constant.

Without energy, nothing can move, vibrate, respond or pulsate. This is a fundamental truth. The energy in an atom and the energy that moves clouds, planets or everything in the universe is the same. Everything that we are aware of can eventually be reduced to energy. So, therefore, energy is omnipresent. It is both visible and invisible. Matter is the visible form of condensed energy, which is the underlying essence of the universe. Life represents the acquisition and expenditure of energy. It cannot exist without the circulation of energy; its very dynamic manifestation depends on energy itself.

Energy cannot pervade the visible and invisible cosmos without consciousness, without an 'awareness' of the laws of nature. These two sides of the cosmos, energy and consciousness, must connect with each other, because all existing entities and materials share a common flow of energy. Without this common energized connection, we would not be able to relate to each other or connect to objects and other species.

Our common energy can be thought of as a common mystic language. We can create a link with anyone or anything in an instant because the core and very root of everything in creation is the same.

There is an attraction between some forms of energy. Gravitational force, being a universal force, for example, is an attractive force. Conscious species can feel that attraction. Philosophically, we may view or experience it as love, because it is an attraction. The nature of this attraction is to keep everyone and everything in balance. It seems, from the perspective of the Universe, that we are indivisible as forms of energy, and we realize and reflect this reality in our desire for the company of humankind. We need reflection; we need to communicate with others in order to experience our own energies and our own conscious presence. This is the essence of attraction.

Attraction is one of the main reasons we want to see people around us, even if we do not talk to them. We may not find psychological rapport, but we do make spiritual connections. These spiritual connections persist, being derived from our connected energy.

People's brain waves vary widely depending on their states of alertness or rest, but the rates of their heartbeats fall more or less within a common range, unless there is a cardiac problem. This is a striking illustration. Beyond the mind, beyond the head or the central nervous system, we possess commonality.

As we descend from the head to the heart, we gradually begin to experience glimpses of the timelessness of the spiritual self. These glimpses may be fleeting, but their positive effects remain as long as we exist physically. The body is time-bound because its very structure is suited to three-dimensional existence. There is a built-in biological clock in our bodies that we cannot override.

In human beings, the pineal gland is situated at the base of the brain and secretes melatonin, acting as a biological clock linked to light and darkness. During darkness, melatonin production is increased by nerve currents and impulses, which are all diverse moments on the same clock. It is thought that melatonin acts to help synchronize the timing of various hormonal glands. It is known that, in animals, this gland also helps in the reproductive cycle. Thus, as the heart beats, the clock is ticking. Our biological clocks keep reminding us of our growth, maturity and age. As if this were not enough, the pineal gland also aids consciousness; indeed, the famous philosopher and mathematician Descartes thought the pineal gland was the seat of the soul. Thus, the function of the pineal gland is sometimes time-bound and sometimes independent of time. All that is physical is time-bound; all that is non-physical, or metaphysical, is timeless. The inner Self is timeless.

Every entity has its own built-in clock. In atoms, an atomic clock can be thought of as ensuring that there is a regular pulsation of electrons. The mind is a psychological clock, a free wheel attached to the physical biological clock; it does not possess a rigid shape or size and it exists to connect and communicate with the many forces that surround our being. The mind can also soar free from the cosmological clock.

There is a rhythm or pattern to the functioning of these clocks. If we do not attune our rhythm to that of others, we experience aversion and discomfort. If we can synchronize our rhythms, we experience oneness. It is easy to discover whether someone can become our good friend or share our rhythm of thinking and living. If we place a hand on a person's chest, while the other person does the same to us, we will be able to conduct an experiment in synchronicity. If we hear and feel a synchronicity of rhythm, we will also experience reflection and oneness. An example of this is the Maori nose greeting, called Hongi, a symbol of trust and unity. 'Ho' is one aspect of breath, while 'Ng' refers to the light aspect of the universal life force. When two people hongi with conscious awareness, they are acknowledging that they are of one breath and catalyse in each other deep healing; they may experience a quickening that opens them up to their higher potential. Another example is the way in which the monthly cycles of women in closed communities often all become synchronous.

Similarly, if our biological and psychological clocks are in tune with the outer environment, we will experience harmony. When music is played we feel uplifted because our hearts are attuned to the beat of the music. As we go on tuning the rhythm of our clock to that of the objects that exist in the universe at various levels, our consciousness expands because we are in tune with many people, many things and many events. Our loneliness or solitude disappears because we see multiple images of ourselves reflected back from many sources. In this way, our thinking and our approach become universal.

Explanations may cause conflicts but experiences do not. Only our senses can create misconceptions or misunderstandings. Once we cross the periphery of the senses, our experiences are universal. As our clocks become more and more synchronized with all that exists around us, our consciousness becomes outside of time. Before we were manifested in our current physical forms, we were timeless, or outside time. When this form of life and existence draws to a conclusion, we will again be timeless. Timelessness and silence are the true nature of the inner Self.

As we become more and more synchronized with all that exists around us, we become timeless in our consciousness.

15

The Nature and Purpose of Energy

Energy as life and creation

The ancients thought of the basic elements of nature as Earth, Water, Fire, Air and Ether and, even today, this is effectively how we experience nature. These elements are all manifestations of different forms of energy sources that have a multitude of effects when interacting with each other. Energy is everywhere, existing at various levels. When a substance dissolves or burns away, energy is released in the breakdown and energy remains in the residue of the substance. Energy is the beginning and the end of everything. Matter is nothing but a compact, compressed form of energy.

Energy is the beginning and the end of every entity.

Knowing this, we need to ask a question: 'What is life?' It is conscious existence, with the acquisition and expenditure of energy, facilitating reproduction. The act of acquiring and expending energy is of a dual nature: conscious and unconscious; voluntary and involuntary.

What then is creation? Energy emanates from one source to another in extraordinary and fascinating ways, going through transformations, transmissions and transitions, which in turn give way to new manifestations of energy. Every particle contains its own energy, just as living beings contain theirs. Energy cannot stay or settle in one location. All entities, whether living or non-living, are subject to the circulation, reception, transmission and diffusion of energy; anything we see serves as a repository of energy in a visible form in that light is absorbed by it or reflected from it. Energy can remain stable only as long as it has no interference with other forms of energy or matter: when it does interact, it will inevitably change or transmute into another form.

The visible universe is full of energy influenced by invisible sources in the cosmos. When we bring the opposite poles of two magnets together, leaving a little space between them, we can feel energy flow through the electromagnetic field and the irresistible pull between the unlike poles. This demonstrates that energy is always being transmitted. All forms of energy, whether visible or invisible, have an 'awareness' of, or we can say are conscious of, their nature, their behaviour, their properties, their progression and regression in relation to one another. Just as human beings are conscious of themselves, their surroundings and other conscious entities, animals are also aware of their surroundings and conscious of themselves and of their friends and foes. They do not have the ability to raise their consciousness as human beings do, unless helped by humans with care and compassion. The powers of reasoning, spoken language and the ability to expand consciousness are the main features that distinguish us from the animal species. Some animals have the ability to learn, adapt and use their previous experience and also have instincts like humans, but they may have little reasoning ability.

Human consciousness is greatly evolved and significantly more refined than the level of consciousness found in non-human species. Hence, we can behave like an animal, an insect or a bird but they cannot behave like us. We have the ability to empathize with and invite the energy of animal beings into our consciousness. Alternatively, we can tune our consciousness to that of any species at its level. We have the capacity of being conscious of ourselves as well as being conscious of everything around us; we are able to recognize and feel various energy patterns. We can raise our consciousness and experience the different flavours and frequencies of energy that exist in nature. No matter how far away the source of energy, we may still be able to connect with it, making space itself a medium of communication because the speed of thought seems to be faster than the speed of light. Light is energy and the light that we have within us that is the spirit of energy may make mystically possible what is physically impossible. We can draw on, taste and experience cosmic energy.

Although the quantitative body is insignificant when compared with the size of the earth, other planets and stars, our spiritual consciousness and thoughts can reach any destination regardless of distance, returning to the source with hitherto unknown information. This transmission of energy can affect particles around us and thus send out the pulses of our wishes, emotions and intuition.

Energy and communication

We have developed sophisticated electronic communications systems such as satellites and mobile phones. We can instantly dial a number and be connected to the internet or to another phone to send or receive information. We have not yet tapped into the deeper resources in our consciousness, however, and what we have achieved in terms of sophisticated communications technology is through the use of just a small portion of our brainpower. We are excited about our current advances. How will we handle the baffling surprises that are yet to come?

There is another level of communication, which is mystical. We use the head as a transmitter, the mind as a satellite and space as the medium. We can target anyone or anything, tune in with the alignment of mind, body and inner spirit and send out thought energies like a magnet aligning particles around it or within it. These phenomena occur in our daily lives but we tend to describe them as mere coincidences or chance.

Spiritual growth is not like physical growth. It is inner growth of a different kind that ignores all the known laws of physics. That is why this highly refined science is called metaphysics. Spiritual growth means bringing our predominantly head-manifested consciousness to the centre of our being, flowing with gravity, whereas physical growth means growing upwards, opposing gravity. Inner consciousness comprehends and experiences outer consciousness in nature, where unity and harmony become part of the same experience.

When we are absorbed in a state of fine intuitive meditation (Dhyana), we can sense the presence of another spiritual person and can follow the advice of our own intuition to reach that person. Not everyone can do this, only those who have developed the intuitive ability to do so through spiritual practice. How does it happen? It is a process that transfers the signals through fine 'particles'. Because our head is fixed as the predominant unit of our body, we often think in a limited way.

The ego that bubbles out to the surface of the mind does not encourage spiritual growth. The head exists in contrast to the heart. Thus we have dual feelings and dual thoughts before we make decisions. The head counsels one course, the heart advises something else and we become confused: 'My heart is whispering, my mind is shouting. Which one do I follow?'

The following hints can help us to discern whether guidance is coming from the mind or the heart:

- The heart speaks when the mind runs out of ideas.
- The heart does not build images but gives us guiding vibrations through our feelings.
- After hearing the whispers of the heart, we feel inspired with the answers that emerge.
- The guidance given by the heart is brief.
- The individual is the only one who can make his or her intuitive feelings guide them.
- If we want to help our hearts speak, we have to observe silence. A serene atmosphere is an advantage.
- The body must be in adequate health and comfort. If one is hungry, thirsty, not feeling well, not surrounded by an atmosphere conducive to guidance, or if one is in a rush or pressured by circumstances, then the heart cannot emit the light of guidance.
- The heart speaks when there is composure in the mind.

Energy and meditation

We all experience something special as we descend into our hearts from our minds. By reducing the excited consciousness in our heads to a composed and ever-peaceful deeper

84

consciousness, we become spiritually aware. We have the gift of changing the atmosphere around us and we are able to sustain the effect of doing so for some time. This innate gift should not be suppressed; it must be explored, exercised and experienced through meditation.

When we blink our eyes, we affect some of the particles near us. This is one of the examples of the effects of energy flow. A major part of our energy is released from the area between the throat and the crown of the head. There is a nexus of many lines of energy communication from our ears, our eyes, our taste buds, our sense of smell and, above all, our sense of touch. This is the reason that, when we lower the excited consciousness from the mind to the composed state of deep-seated inner consciousness, we experience peace.

Experiencing peace means experiencing a balanced state of energy within us. This is the first benefit one achieves by meditating. If we can withdraw the engagement of our consciousness from the senses with the help of that same mind, we will feel energy brimming over.

In traditional Eastern philosophy, the mind is likened to a crazed and drunken monkey bitten by a scorpion. It often regrets incidents. We usually begin to analyse these incidents after they occur and make resolutions that we will change, but again we stumble, if not in the same situation, then in different circumstances or on a different issue. Sometimes we become frustrated by our own natures and by our behaviour and reaction to others. Eventually we become pessimistic about personal improvement and progress. Rarely do we find a true reflection of our minds in others. Our intellects engage in relentless analysis until we lose our sense of peace. Then there dawns upon us an urge to remain silent and solitary and to meditate in a state of being where the heart blossoms, consoles and soothes the mind, bringing vision, guidance and intuitive direction.

First, there is experience, then explanation. Experience endorses explanation, thereby making explanation authentic. One's explanations can be refuted but one cannot deny true inner experiences as they are testimonials that leave a lasting impression.

Energy can be transmitted or absorbed wilfully from oneself. Released energy is like an arrow shot from the centre of one's being, while energy that is absorbed is like rain coming from the heights of nature onto the depths of consciousness. The conscious act of releasing and absorbing energy requires consistent practice and unswerving dedication. For example, to become a great painter, one may have to dedicate one's entire life to art. To become a qualified professional, one may have to spend a lifetime in pursuit of knowledge and still not be able to perfect one's skill. Likewise, in order to reach a certain level of personal and internal growth, one needs to devote time to explore, experience and bring out the treasures of one's inner self.

Some people, who have no knowledge of meditation, may say that anyone can sit and meditate. They presume that meditation is for those who are elderly or retired, or have little else serious to occupy them. Although spiritual enlightenment should be one of the highest objectives of human life, we have ignored this major goal and have used the lens of the mind to magnify minor targets. Increasingly, we create artificial requirements and ignore the real necessities of our lives. In the course of fulfilling our material needs, we may become insensitive to the comforts around us.

We constantly derive energy from different sources, such as the sun, plants and trees, the atmosphere, water, food and drink, animal species and people. We relentlessly expend this same energy whether we are conscious or unconscious of it. At every exhalation, at every pulsing of the nerves and with every beat of the heart, there is energy loss. Thinking, feeling, speaking, hearing, smelling – whatever the nature of the act, there is always an expenditure of energy.

Energy and spirituality

Life means experiencing the gain and loss of energy through our bodies and our consciousness, retaining the impressions of beauty, truth and love, the first a surface experience of life and the second a balanced experience. Most people live a shallow life. They know they are missing something, but they do not know what. Some people keep themselves very busy to avoid inquiring further, since they have consciously or unconsciously cultivated their egos, supported by dry rationalization. Some people look good, work hard, make money and may even be famous, yet they do not have the experience of deeper life. Looking good is different from being good. Working hard does not necessarily mean one is efficient, making money does not mean one is rich, being famous does not mean one is great.

People with spiritual awareness live a deeper life. They live every moment, keeping their minds and hearts open to learning and new experiences. The ability to empathize is greater in such people than in those without spiritual awareness. They breathe consciously and experience altered states of consciousness. They live deeply through the dreaming, waking and sleeping states of consciousness. They are sensitive to different energy patterns.

With their meditative ability they can reduce or increase the acquisition and expenditure of energy. Energy is more subtle than we realize. It brings awareness, clarity, understanding, wisdom and enlightenment. It provides the ability to become attuned to a person with whom one has had no previous acquaintance. People around those with spiritual awareness experience a positive effect merely from being in their presence. Some feel better just by speaking to them. Others experience a sense of relief from discomfort, or achieve transformation by the release of their energies, thoughts, wishes, words and presence.

This can have a tremendous effect on the lives of others and happens as a result of a spiritual evolution of consciousness. Wishes that are made casually or superficially do not materialize. The thinking process of the inner operator must go on deepening every day. For example, if you keep thinking 'I am not good', you will certainly begin to experience the negative effect of these thoughts and words. Repetition of the mantra-like phrases 'I am bad' and 'I am not good' lead you into precisely that experience, since the negative energy you generate rebounds on you like a boomerang.

The same effect can also be seen in the case of hatred or vengeance. In that situation, the energy generated travels with the traces of the image one intends towards a person and the released energy goes in search of the person until a match is found. Distance has little role to play when it comes to thought or energy transmission. Whatever the nature of the particular thought, its originator becomes the first target or victim in the case of negative thoughts and the first beneficiary of positive thoughts. Because of this principle in nature, most of us think twice before we hurt others, as subconsciously we are aware that we will reap what we sow.

Spiritually evolved people are able to align their states of consciousness, altering their energy levels, attuning and communicating with nature, thus bringing tremendous effective energy into their beings and then distributing it to others.

We can draw in energy from a flower, a plant, an animal or a person in many different ways: through touch, through the eyes, through breathing, through our hearts, and through our will and deeper consciousness. Similarly we can send out energy, using any instrument of energy transmission. As energy is the finest form of universal expression, there is no mechanical technique involved in the act and process. Operational techniques are within our reach and will. Open-mindedness, genuine interest to learn and experiment, are vitally important.

The mind can be taught to accept, by being receptive and inviting images, information, inspiration and energy into one's consciousness so that one gains mystical experiences of non-physical truth.

The pause between inhalation and exhalation is life.

Human life is governed by two main forces: a positive (constructive) force and a negative (destructive) force. Life can never be one-sided; it is always a combination of construction and destruction. We are experiencing this at every moment and with every breath. When we breathe in, we do so through a constructive force, and when we breathe out, we exhale through a negative force. The pause between inhalation and exhalation is an experience of subtle life force. The time between the past and the future is life. Every moment some cells are born, while others die. Where the two forces act, both are energy but the effects are two-fold, i.e. positive and negative. When we wish something for somebody, we have to unify our energy fields with theirs, ignoring all differences and becoming tuned into oneness, innocence and forgiveness. Only then will the wish be powerful enough to help others with their well-being or fulfilment.

We must dilute the negative influences and impressions of the past, by enhancing and focusing more on a positive understanding of events gone by. If we can heighten our awareness and expand our consciousness individually, our perceptions change and we broaden our thinking. With these changes, negativity and misunderstanding are washed away with the flood of compassion. Thus, we can change the world collectively, making the earth greener, safer and more beautiful.

VI

THE UNIVERSE

The universe challenges the imagination and humbles the ego

16

Cosmic Evolution

Light is good but blinding light is not good. Love is good but binding love is not good.

The earth and the sun can be thought of as our galactic parents, earth being our mother and the sun our father. Mother earth's love manifests itself as gravity, her compassion in oceans and her caring nature in green vegetation. Mother earth is of immaculate beauty. She stands as a unique example of endurance. She always forgives our mischief against her. Though we often trouble her in the name of research, discovery or progress, her love for her children endures. Mother earth is beneath our feet, but we barely appreciate her or her infinite compassion.

Just as biological mothers generate milk in their breasts to feed their children, mother earth produces plants and vegetation for us to survive. And the galactic father of us all, the sun, remains high in the sky – working relentlessly, burning with light and energy to bring warmth to all species. Yet, despite their sacrifices, we scarcely recognize our cosmic parents.

Fire, water and air are our nearest imaginable relatives. They all have a close connection with one another. All planets and satellites of planets are our paternal relatives. Stars and other celestial bodies are our distant cosmic relatives.

Parents want to discipline their children but children wish to be loved unconditionally. Love and discipline seldom unite successfully. Our bodily systems, the rhythms of our physical functions, are highly disciplined because they have been perfectly engineered by nature. As long as our heartbeats, body temperatures and blood counts are strictly regulated, we are well. If our physical bodies were not disciplined, we would not be able to survive even for a few minutes. By contrast, the inner spirit that operates the physical body is flowing and free of the rigid disciplinary rules of nature. Our imaginations soar far above the visible universe, without restraint.

Creation has yielded a marvellous combination: the earthly body and the cosmic spirit, the rational mind and the loving heart.

Coming to terms with this dichotomy in our own lives is a valuable and educational adventure.

Our day of birth is when we manifest ourselves on the planet. Many ask themselves, or others, 'What happens after death?' The question could be rephrased as, 'What happened before birth?' After being born, we are aware that we exist. We find the reality of existence astonishing: how we breathe, how we live, how we form societies and communicate with each other – reality is complex and remarkable. Is it not wonderful to contemplate the plain truth that nothing is more intriguing than the human mind, body and consciousness? Though we are all different in the way we think and act, we communicate with one another through a common platform of society and we share our thoughts, opinions and views. The happiest news is that we are conscious, that we exist, and that we are in a spacious universe and not a cage.

Our intuition whispers that, internally, we are eternal. Externally, or physically speaking, we are mortals. We all want to live for ever in perfect youthful health and beauty. At every age, we possess this same inner desire. But why do we want something so contrary to the laws of nature? The cosmic answer is quite simple: we long to return to the state we were in before confining ourselves to a physical body as human beings. Being immaculately beautiful and perfect is our true state of existence. Thus, desiring to be the same while existing in a physical body is an evolutionary phase. This stage of the creation of the whole cosmos is not complete. It is in its infancy. Recent studies in astronomy and astrophysics indicate that the universe is still expanding. There are many more things to be discovered in the course of this growth that will improve our quality of life. These discoveries will take place as universal consciousness expands and blossoms further.

We have advanced so far over the course of time, and evolved so much from our original state of existence. In our infancy as a species, we were struck down by minor ailments. In this century, we have not only developed cures for conditions that frightened us in the past, but we have also come to learn of unexpected benefits from what we previously regarded as threats.

Similarly, a century ago we only dreamed of flight, which is now a reality. More recently, we have begun to dream of colonizing the moon and Mars. The pace of our development and our achievements is astonishing. Concomitantly, there has never been as much interest in spirituality as we see today. There is an ever-growing fascination with metaphysics, mysticism, complementary medicine, alternative philosophies, hyperphysics, mind dynamics, and spiritual study and experience. At this stage of our evolution we can only imagine how much more we will learn of humanity, nature and the universe in the future.

We define ourselves as human beings and are conscious of our origin, being and true nature. Because we are conscious of our physical existence, we believe that that is all there is. Because of the limitations of our senses and our rational minds, we know of no existence beyond this plane.

However, existence is a continuum and a perpetual law of the universe. If death and dissolution are certain, birth and re-emergence must also be certain. We must journey much further within our consciousness to understand the true nature of our existence, and to experience it in full. Only then will we be able to understand some of the greatest secrets of nature. Mysticism and spirituality, rather than merely explaining physical existence, lead us to different dimensions of the conscious universe.

We emerged from the universe, we exist in the universe and we will continue to be in the universe. *We are more than we think we are. We are more than we believe we are.* Existence to existence is a cosmic dance, a wave of consciousness. Birth and death are just the beginning and end of a wave of life in the ocean of infinite life-consciousness.

We should celebrate this spiritual truth: that we existed before, we exist now and shall exist tomorrow and forever, in many ways, in different forms at different times. We should have boundless gratitude to nature for giving us the opportunity to experience so many forms of existence in the cosmos.

After all, if we were to live for thousands of years only in this body, how awkward life would be. We would suffer countless injuries, carry an overload of information and bear memories, or unpleasant images, that would not let us sleep or rest. We would have set ways of thinking and not have the possibility to exist anew. Life would be stale and stagnant. Evolution, which refines every new generation, would slow down. The whole cosmos would look humdrum. Thus we owe tremendous thanks to the cosmic forces that brought us into existence, entertaining us with illusions and reality, light and darkness, physicality and spirituality, birth and death, ignorance and enlightenment.

Our birthday does not just represent our day of birth. It is a day of celebration for all those related and connected to us, and for all the elements of nature present within us. Our birthday is the day we registered our human awareness in the consciousness of the universe.

17

Beyond the Physical

'I am in the universe' is a physical fact.
'The universe is in me' is a spiritual truth.
'I am the universe' is a mystical experience.

'I am in the universe' is a physical reality. 'The universe is in me' is a spiritual reality. The former relegates us to the position of insignificant beings in the infinitude of nature. The latter reality renders us as significant conscious beings. 'I am in the universe' is exciting. 'The universe is in me' is fulfilling.

This spiritual reality is re-established and revived through personal experience. Our awareness is in-between the outer universal self and the inner self. Our consciousness can be projected either inwardly or outwardly by our will and personal endeavour. Outward projection is scientific; inward projection is spiritual.

We begin to see and experience the parallel universe that is outside ourselves. We extend more of our consciousness and energy to experience only a physical reality. The notion 'I am in the universe' multiplies our endless questions and entangles us in a maze, where only a few questions are answered and more questions arise. 'The universe is in me' leads to fewer questions, but more experience.

Experience of the inner universe becomes possible by penetrating the various resistant strata of our inner consciousness, where intellect, initially a hindrance because of its questioning nature, serves as a cursor to lead the surface-conscious awareness from the mind to the heart, to the innermost expanses of consciousness, to the core of the Self. This is a mystically adventurous journey, a meditative process, a *Dhyana* grace.

What we feel, see and experience within can also be manifested outside us. Although the universe is common to us all, we perceive it in different ways because the level of conscious evolution varies among individuals. Duality serves to explain countless examples in nature. An example is wave particle duality, when sometimes phenomena, such as electron diffraction, are best explained by treating particles as waves. In a different way, we can regard the ocean as water and as waves. Physical reality is more or less the same throughout our range of perception, whereas inner experiences of the universe, through our consciousness, are unique. We possess individual, unique universes within us.

When we get to the very core of being we are all the same. As we move from our core-self to the heart and mind, we gradually begin to see differences and individualities with unique natures and qualities. We experience the universe in a myriad of different ways.

A spiritually advanced person sees everything with his or her heart, using intuition more than intellect. Rational thinkers sharpen their intellect on the physical reality of the universe, but ignore much beneath this. Eventually they realize what they have missed in their lives as a result of focusing on the analysis of outer reality only. Intellectual pursuits alone are never truly fulfilling. Both inner and outer exploration should be pursued in combination, or preference should be given to learning more of what is within us.

The notion that 'the universe is in me' becomes a greater spiritual reality as we elevate our consciousness through personal endeavour and sincere inquiry. This type of quest brings enlightenment. We can unify physical and spiritual reality into an absolute experience of the self. 'I am in the universe' has less oneness and more separation. 'The universe is in me' conveys no separation. We find oneness in our existence, the visible universe and everything that occurs outside us.

Whether we see, hear, taste or feel, it is all from the inner self. The physical senses are only tools. Our eyes may be open but we still may not be seeing because the inner self may not have connected to the sensory organs.

Many things happen on the surface, at the level of the mind, which echo the inner self in various patterns. Experiencing one's inner self through spirituality is also to experience something outside of oneself. We can transmit our experiences through touch and emotion and sometimes by silence. Our words limit us from achieving the subtle experience of the inner universe.

Scientific understanding is impersonal. Spiritual experience is personal.

Dhyana leads one to the experience of the inner universe or the inner spiritual reality. Spiritual reality is the foundation of physical reality but our perceptions reverse this truth. Though the universe is common to all of us, everyone's perceived universe is unique. Hence we have many things to share with each other. Each time we listen to someone's experiences, we are surprised by newly discovered truths.

We are all working collectively, consciously and unconsciously, to live a better life. We are trying to understand more about nature, our resources and the way nature operates. We try to become more aware of our presence in the world and to become enlightened about the truth of our existence and the truth of the cosmos. We have various belief systems and various perceptions of the universe. The process of achieving higher consciousness is an ongoing one. We attempt to reach it from different angles, like trying to reach the summit of a mountain from different directions. If we are truly dedicated to our objective, we end up at the place of our choosing, and this is a place of enlightenment.

18

Journeying between the Outer and the Inner Realms

Although the human mind is a subject of study, the mysticism of the mind has not been much experienced or widely understood. It is intriguing that the morphological structure and physiological functions of the brain are more or less the same in every human being, but the nature, attitude and perceptions of the mind are starkly different in each individual.

We exist physically in three dimensions and we are also subject to the dimensions of time and space, but our real deeper consciousness begins at the fifth dimension where feelings prevail and intuition sparks, inviting us to explore infinite dimensions of mystical and spiritual experiences with which we start to perceive the world far more clearly than before.

We are fifth-dimensional beings as we live mainly through our feelings, imagination, intuition and experiences.

Sleep is a pause between the waking and the dream. We understand many things without reading or listening, the traditional methods of learning. Our existence is in the middle of both the inner and outer universes. The outer universe is characterized by a rational approach and experiences are gained through the senses and the physical body. The experience of the inner universe occurs primarily through intuition, the heart, the emotional self and the spiritual self. When we view the world from a logical perspective, we all understand it in the same way. However, when the perception of the world reaches our core, it is different from what others may perceive and it is also somewhat different from what we ourselves perceived previously.

At the level of the heart, everyone is in oneness and oneness is in everyone.

The outer universe is physical, whereas our individual inner universe is a reflective experience of the same outer universe at either the microcosmic or macrocosmic level. The process of experiencing the inner universe is spiritual. It is a personal experience. As we go deeper into our inner being, we realize oneness. We all have the choice whether to progress in reaching the outer universe or in exploring the inner universe. The process of reaching the outer universe with our consciousness, with our intellectual and physical resources, is scientific and systematic. The process of reaching the depths of our inner universe is spiritual and inspirational.

We cannot access both the inner and outer universes equally in life. We are always pulled more towards one or the other. Though we all have a similar physical brain, we have trained our minds to progress in a particular field of study, such as art, medicine, philosophy or economics. We cannot gain mastery over all subjects equally. If we progress only towards reaching the outer universe, we grow intellectually. We increase the quantity of information in our brains, but we may feel emptiness. If we attempt to descend into the inner universe, we may be criticized by people who have progressed in the material sense. However, as we discover the depths of the inner universe, we feel contentment, satisfaction and the elevation of our spirits.

Our physical body is local (physical presence restricted to one location), but, spiritually, we are gifted with the ability to become non-local, with our consciousness hardly affected by our local physical presence. This is a mystical experience. We travel in many directions with our thoughts. After a while we return to our main co-ordinate, the physical body.

Cells within our body function individually, yet they contribute collectively to our body's overall activity. Every cell within the body has its own magnitude of consciousness. We have discovered exquisite intracellular mechanisms of genetic coding in our DNA, as well as a vast array of cellular receptors and intercellular messenger molecules, which are thought to facilitate cellular function. However, each cell is powered in essence by the spirit within us.

Similarly our inner universes are powered by universal consciousness. When we communicate only on an intellectual level, we often end up misunderstanding or misinterpreting others. When human communication is embellished by the touch of our hearts, then clarity, harmony and oneness can be found. We can only feel oneness in the universe, oneness with everyone, when we gaze spiritually from our inner universe. Younger children experience oneness regardless of their backgrounds. People who are advanced in age experience the same oneness that children do because the level of consciousness is the same at the two extremes of life. There is conflict between these stages, but newborn babies, young children and people of advanced age live mainly in their inner universe.

As we descend into the depths of the inner universe, we embrace the outer universe simultaneously. If we descend one micro-millimetre into the inner universe, our understanding and perception of the outer universe extends thousands of miles. This is the scale of our spiritual journey. Keeping in touch with our inner Self through silence, meditation or *Dhyana is only to reassure us that we are progressing.* Once we are consciously aware of our true nature, we will continue to evolve. As we gain experiences on the journey, we will become more confident of our inner treasure. We can brighten up the light of our spirits with our will. The effects of this mystical light can then be observed by others.

VII

NATURE

Expression without inhibition

19

Visible and Invisible Nature

We have been blessed by nature with various faculties, capabilities and powers. We have been well equipped with abundant resources such as intellect, memory, imagination, individual will and, above all, mystical and spiritual faculties. There is a super-sensor, a deep-seated self beneath everything we feel, think and talk about, which embodies the impenetrable formulas, codes and secrets of nature and the universe; just as genes in the body carry information about our ancestors. These physical, mystical and spiritual resources are bestowed upon us so that we can explore either our inner consciousness of the self or our outer consciousness of the universe. Perhaps it is the will of nature for us to exist in this way and to endeavour to realize our potential and our internal riches. We struggle against the temptations of the world and the resistance posed by other forces in nature to succeed in exploring life, consciousness and the universe and thus to become enlightened beings.

We can see the world, we can hear the world, we can taste the world and we can feel the world. We can explore our life and consciousness from various directions. We are not gifted with only one kind of sense. We have five main senses, but with deeper understanding and experience of the human body, we realize that there are many other senses. For example, we have a sense that can feel pressure, or weight, and we have senses that detect temperature. As we progress in our research, we will discover many things about our bodies that we cannot comprehend at this time.

We are well prepared by nature to explore life and consciousness. There is a higher force guiding us that is invisible. Our bodies are visible because we exist in the visible universe, which can also be called nature. Hence, we experience the beauty of nature.

Visible nature emerges out of invisible nature. It is a manifestation of the laws of nature. What we call invisible nature has a deeper connection with our invisible inner spirit, or invisible inner consciousness, while visible nature encourages us to develop our intelligence and invites us to understand nature's behaviour.

We have translated our philosophical and theoretical knowledge about visible nature into practical benefits such as science and technology. Invisible nature, however, inspires us to experience ourselves. Invisible nature, being the basis of visible nature, inspires us to develop our intuition so that we can connect with it, consciously or unconsciously, and take or absorb mystical guidance in order to make our lives more meaningful, more satisfying and more significant.

When we drive or walk, we know whether to turn left or right, or simply to go forward, in order to reach our destination, but here is a life-path different from the visible path. The latter is a common road that all may journey on and thus we have common rules decreeing, for example, that we must all drive on the right or on the left. But each individual's *life*-path is unique.

Our life-paths are mystical. One person cannot show another his or her life-path. Each person has to see their own life-path for themself. And one's life-path can only be seen clearly with the help of higher visions, or with the help of invisible nature. In the daily routine of life, we use our common sense or logic. We use our knowledge and experience to avoid difficulties, to make our lives smooth and uncomplicated. However, when everything else has been tried and exhausted, when nothing is clearly visible, we are fortunate and very much blessed because we can use our intuition to connect with higher invisible nature.

Intuition is a flashlight; it does not glow all the time. Intuition pulsates, or flashes from the heart. Intuition and intelligence may exist in parallel, but cannot function simultaneously. When we are engaged in using our intelligence, our intuition recedes. When we allow our intuition to whisper, intelligence sleeps because the same consciousness manifests itself in different ways, in different regions of the body, at different times. Wherever we direct our will and focus, that part of the body manifests greater consciousness.

If we are suffering from physical discomfort, we seek medical help. We undergo physical examination and diagnosis. Even if doctors do not find a major problem, we have still experienced pain or discomfort that we cannot diagnose by ourselves. The experience of pain is real; the sensation is real and we worry about how to overcome it. Our thoughts deepen, we reach the edge of thought and begin to enter the realm of feeling. Here we become attuned with the invisible forces that guide all species. Then we are led through dreams, or through an image in our thoughts that provides inspiration, or we have a spontaneous experience that brings us the right solution or the appropriate guidance. Intuition becomes the medium of such higher communication.

VIII

CONSCIOUSNESS

Moving clouds of thoughts in the sky of consciousness

20

Consciousness beyond Science

In the truest sense we still do not know who we really are. We find ourselves pondering these questions:

- How much potential do we have?
- What is our true identity and role in this vast universe?
- Does the universe belong exclusively to us, or are there extraterrestrial beings out there, perhaps far more advanced than we are?
- If there are alien beings, do they share the same universe?
- What about other universes that have not yet engaged our imagination?

When we observe human history, we see that we have always shown evolutionary progress in our thinking. We have changed the world into something that is quite different from what it was before. It is evident that there are incredible changes still to occur in our thinking, living and interaction with the world. As time passes, we find ourselves changed by new discoveries and inventions. In the process of evolution the time perceived by us is just a second in the infinitude of space and the universe. In order for us to evolve minutely in the expansion of our consciousness, it may take hundreds of thousands of years.

Beneath our known consciousness, there is unconscious awareness that we are unable to access readily. Only when we minimize the expenditure of our energy by being in silence for a while, are we able to sense our latent unconsciousness.

Whatever today's scientific psychological studies about human consciousness have revealed, it is merely surface knowledge, although it has been acquired through years of research. Disciplined scientific study grants us clearer understanding of the facts on any given subject, but, when it comes to studying human consciousness, we have to adopt an alternative method if we wish to encompass the invisible truths of our own nature and our unconscious.

This round-about, mystical approach accesses our inner realms of consciousness through silent meditation and by exploring the deeper folds of consciousness with the cursor of the mind. Conscious awareness adds more meaning to life.

We can liken the physical body to a flower. Imagine a flower with five petals, as we have five senses. The nature of a flower is captured in its softness and sensitivity. Similarly, the heart is a sensitive organ and, when we draw a picture of a heart, it resembles a flower or a leaf. A flower usually has fragrance, as does the heart, which emits the fragrance of love. The flower's fragrance extends beyond its physical boundaries. In much the same manner, the fragrance of love from a blossoming human heart spreads beyond the boundaries of the physical being, inspiring others whose creative hearts have not yet blossomed.

Memory is first stored in the brain and, with time, as newer information enters our brain, the previously deep stored memory is gradually filtered and funnelled through the throat region and settles somewhere in the heart. This has yet to be fully understood. In this process the heart retains the essence and leaves out

113

everything else. This is one of the reasons why, when part of the brain is damaged in a person as a result of an accident or for other reasons, the person still manages to live a normal life without the loss of memory, because memory stored deep in the heart is reprocessed and sent up to the remaining part of the brain. As we grow older, we lose a large number of neurons, yet the loss is compensated by deeper memory stored in the heart. However, the whole memory is not stored in the brain alone; impressions of the memory are reflected throughout the body. Each cell carries a particular kind of memory. This is how DNA molecules in a cell can have so much memory about its ancestors. People who are emotional usually possess a good memory. When they become emotional at another time, they reawaken the memory from the heart and bring it to the surface of the mind.

The human heart is like the heart of the universe, and hence it is sacred. Unfolding the petals of one's heart means gaining access to the secrets of the universe.

Without disturbing the flow of our lives, our hearts can store subtle memories in a manner that has yet to be unravelled by science. If we were to store all our experiences only in terms of digital information in our neurons, we would not experience peace and love because our minds would suffer an excess of information. This overload could trigger memories that would affect the flow of our thoughts and our words.

Fortunately, our experiences become profoundly subtle as they transcend our being and are finally transformed into subtle energies entering the deeper recesses of our bodies and our consciousness. The essence of all our memories and experiences adds something to our auric fields. These are the fields that we radiate, which are magnetic, mystical, embracing and transformational in nature. The auric field of a person can affect the cellular activity in another person in either positive or negative ways. Thus every person's thoughts and words are more important than their deeds. Deeds are only an infinitesimal expression of our thoughts. The effect we have on others returns to affect us.

Each human being must be looked upon as an inspiration to the world. The underlying principle of the universe is that goodness in us inspires goodness in others.

Everybody is directly related to the earth, and hence its magnetic field has a profound influence on our bodies. It is also the reason why we feel a strong relationship with some places that are new to us. In some places, regardless of the good environment, we feel depressed. In other places, we can meditate and feel better, even if we are recovering from sickness. Our metaphysical energy fields are continuously affected by the auric fields that we experience and possibly also by the earth's magnetic field, but it is possible to maintain a certain degree of balance in our own energy levels.

Many people experience different states of consciousness and different emotions, such as anger, peace and joy, when they travel to different places because the earth's magnetic field varies from region to region. This happens even when they have little awareness of where they are. In spite of this, if we meditate, we can be less affected and it is possible for us to maintain a certain degree of balance in our own energy levels.

The underlying principle of the universe is that goodness in us inspires goodness in others. However, because a person may not have resources, such as knowledge, courage and endurance, to communicate with those who show a negative response, their goodness may provoke another person to become negative and sometimes destructive towards the person with goodness. This response occurs because the other person feels that their beliefs and existence are threatened. If goodness is communicated effectively, then it can transform and inspire the goodness latent in the hearts of everyone. This is reflected in our auric fields, which act like shields, like cosmic protection that is similar to the skin's protection of the body. Whether the forces outside us are destructive or constructive by nature, they first have to penetrate our metaphysical-auric energy fields.

These energy fields can be likened to radiant energy both within and outside an electric light bulb. We can sense another person's energy with our heart. Even if our eyes are closed or blindfolded, our hearts are still able to divine whether that person's energy is positive or negative. This is because the conscious body is full of vibrations and energy. The waves that emanate from the centre of a person are of two kinds, or two different natures; one attracts, while the other repels.

When we stand near a person or walk into a person's periphery and focus, we can *feel* or sense whether we should remain there or should leave. If the waves of consciousness radiating from a person are beneficial to our existence, we feel like remaining and extending the conversation. Although the person may wish to leave us, we still wish to prolong our time with them. Upon returning home we feel a sense of elation and an increase of energy. Even though we have not had a meal, we feel very strong. We have been inspired in the presence of that person's metaphysical–auric energy field. We have reawakened our own energies, as a result of the influence of the energy of that person.

Until now, science has rarely touched upon this topic, because it is beyond the range of the physical senses. A great deal of scrutiny and dedication is required to understand this experience. Currently, science focuses on practical technology and materials that can be measured by physical means. It will eventually move on to other areas of human existence. As advances are made in genetics, microbiology, nanotechnology, astrophysics and quantum physics, science and technology are gradually becoming less obviously related to the physical world as we experience it. In the past, psychology has branched out and become more specialized. Humanistic psychology, including cognitive understanding, social psychology and even parapsychology are some of its branches. These developments indicate that we are opening our minds to learn more about ourselves. We are travelling on two tracks and one day there will be a point of convergence, where psychologists, mystics and physicists will meet. *Yet, no matter what we manage to explain or establish through scientific means, the fulfilment of an individual's life potential is only possible through spiritual experience.*

Experience is for ourselves. Explanation is for others. We cannot experience for others; we can only help them achieve experience. We can create a platform for others to experience something, but we cannot experience it on their behalf. We *can*, however, relate to others. We can tune ourselves to different levels, we can master the art of tuning our energies and consciousness to different individuals, with whom we will then have greater ability to empathize.

Every entity in the universe has its own aura of existence. There are two facets of existence: physical and metaphysical. When we omit the prefix 'meta', we refer to physical existence. 'Meta' means *beyond* and metaphysics is concerned with experience beyond logical understanding. This is similar to psychology and parapsychology (where 'para' also means beyond). For example, a rock has a physical appearance, yet has its own field of existence in a metaphysical sense. It has 'consciousness', that is, the laws of nature that brought it to its present state are embedded within it in a way that is more than physical. Thus, it has its own destiny and origin. It has its own process of evolution, having broken away from a huge rock or mountain, or perhaps it has been worn away or simply dissolved in water over time. A rock is 'conscious', but its consciousness is at a low level in the universe. Humans, in contrast, exist at the highest level of consciousness on the planet, while animals, plants and minerals are at intermediate levels of consciousness. The earth as a whole is highly conscious.

Before we touch an object with our hands, if we are sensitive enough, we can feel the presence of that object. We can feel its auric field when we are close to it. We can embrace it with our field of existence by extending our consciousness and energy. We have reached a halfway point. Touching with the hand is then only a physical attestation or confirmation. Using our consciousness to touch objects is an advanced experience.

Animals and plants are not as 'conscious' of their existence as we are. Plants and trees are fixed in one place, but they do have their own invisible fields of existence. Animals can explore their potential in the same way as humans. Whales, for example, are born with innate intelligence, but, with the help of human training, they can develop that intelligence and achieve greater possibilities. Monkeys, dogs, horses, cats, elephants and many other animals can also be trained, as can birds such as parrots and pigeons. In the past, birds have performed a postman's job. They carried mail very efficiently, maintaining their altitude in a particular direction, overcoming the dangers of flight, travelling to specific destinations and delivering messages to the intended recipients.

Whether animal, human being or any other entity, if we are inspired, if our existence is significantly reflected in others and if we become conscious of our inner capabilities and potentials, we can raise our consciousness in all directions.

Our physical existence is like an atom where 'I-ness' (I am) is the nucleus of our consciousness. In the case of an atom, the nucleus constitutes virtually the entire mass of that atom. The rest of the atom consists of electrons that surround the nucleus in a cloud made up of a series of orbits. Similarly, there are many layers of 'electron' orbits that surround the nucleus of 'I-awareness'. These include the emotional and psychological layers, and layers created by the conditioning of our minds. Through spiritual experiences, we become conscious of 'I-ness'. By elevating our consciousness, we make our energy more 'magnetic' and positive. When we reach that stage, people around us feel uplifted.

If waves of energy emanating from our being are beneficial to our existence and are of a positive nature, those waves will also be beneficial to others. Those who walk into our auric fields will have more or less the same experience as we do. Our metaphysical–auric energy fields form a mystical circle around us.

119

Technology has greatly improved in recent years and can now capture this 'something' that surrounds us. We call it a nimbus, halo, an aura or an energy field.

21

The Manifestation of Consciousness

All living beings are aware of their existence but it is only human beings who are aware and conscious of their capabilities. In particular, humans are the only beings endowed with the power of reasoning and the ability to express their feelings, thoughts and emotions with refined intelligence.

There is energy everywhere but the guidance for every being and every celestial body, whether a star, a planet, a comet or even an atom, comes from the highest, intelligent consciousness. This energy is simply in everything and everything is in it, but the resources, longevity and destination of every existence can only be guided by consciousness, which is everywhere, from sub-atomic particles to giant heavenly bodies. If there is no consciousness, nothing moves in order and nothing moves in rhythm. Every being has a definable function and pattern, and an indefinable nature.

When we open our eyes, we are more in the mind. When we close our eyes, we are more in the heart. In this swing between the mind and the heart, we are the same conscious being, but when our eyes are open our internal conscious existence becomes minute. During this time, our conscious awareness spreads out externally. When we close our eyes with the intention of embracing the feeling heart, serenity prevails, peace surrounds us and a deep feeling of oneness occurs within.

Creation is both visible and invisible. The visible part of creation is like the body of a universal conscious entity. The invisible portion of creation is the spirit of infinite consciousness in the cosmos. As anything is possible in our minds and imaginations, so too anything becomes possible in the mind of the cosmic consciousness.

When our eyes are open, we experience more of our presence in the world and we become more vulnerable. We can be easily disturbed by the looks and thoughts of others, since our inner spiritual strength starts to dissipate. Whereas, when our eyes are closed wilfully and consciously, we reawaken our inner spiritual strength and feel that all that is within us is unified and hence protected. We also feel more of our life force present in the body.

The mind is the magic of human life; if there is no mind, there is no magic, there is no entertainment, there is no excitement. The mind is a kaleidoscope. We see so many colours and flavours, and so many forms of the same universe. The mind creates endless multiple images, to the extent that we become restless.

Sleep is one of the most indispensable gifts to living beings. We sleep well when the body has been exercised. Our brains are wearied by constant thinking, resisting and responding to unceasing stimuli from the world outside. As a result of this activity, the mind recedes and sleep takes over. Dreams are an interruption of the sub-conscious mind, stirring deep-seated emotional memories, impressions of images expressed and unexpressed. During sleep our cells become recharged because they have low cellular activity. Sleep recharges our cells. Many people, though they have luxury and comfort, cannot sleep; they take medication to help them. They may not be inspired to journey from a thinking mode to the feeling heart. They may not know the art of descending internally from the troubled mind to the serene heart. They may have no confidence in their metabolism, the body's automatic repair system, capable of producing certain chemicals that make us sleep.

Meditation, with the observance of certain mystic gestures, is a natural way of reviving the body, mind and spirit. You can try the following. Oppose the right thumb and the forefinger, but keep the rest of the fingers close to one another. Bring the hand over the chest and internalize the mind. Keep your eyes closed to increase energy and focus on the gesture. Gradually deepen your breath in both exhalation and inhalation. Dwell on the touch of the chest with the gesture. Deepen your wish to experience the meditative state of consciousness. Then you will begin to feel unity, oneness and the centralization of the extensions of your being. Something profound and graceful happens in us at the centre of our hearts.

We realize the limitation of words when our experiences are profound.

If you lie down for a few minutes after this exercise and then examine your face in a mirror, you will be able to judge for yourself the effectiveness of meditation.

Consciousness as a wave

The universe is in motion. It dances, with all the stars and planets moving in elliptical orbits. It moves in a beautiful artistic wave. Mystics can experience it.

The mind is there to entertain us. If we want entertainment, we have to be present more in the mind. We swing between the mind and the heart. The mind tends towards materialism, looking for novelties for its occupation, and if these are not found we fall asleep. Keep on repeating a sentence or a word with a monotonous tone, and we may exhibit a degree of attention at first, but after a few minutes we will show signs of boredom. Eventually we may become drowsy and fall asleep. Indeed we often count sheep to help us fall asleep. Alternatively, we may become irritated and angry. While a person may become immune to such repetition, it is the nature and weakness of the human mind to become bored or depressed by a repetitive stimulus.

We need to examine who or what we are. Sometimes we are the mind, sometimes we are the heart and at other times we are the spirit. However, we are never purely the body, because we recognize our physical existence only when we are conscious.

After busy and noisy activities the mind becomes tired and the heart awakens. We become receptive and humble. We have no negativity and there is no competition or envy. We re-experience innocence because we are more in the heart. We realize that we are superior to what we thought we were. We embrace ourselves. We understand more by pausing in our activities. If we suffer any minor injury, we do not notice at that moment because, as outsiders, we are not aware of what is happening to the body.

When we finish work, we regain our awareness of the body. We experience consciousness in our hearts because we have returned to our homes. The mind does not perturb us as much because we have given sustenance to the mind and the body. The mind now settles and the body is comforted. The heart is soothed. Our consciousness expands and we experience peace. We have shaken off heaviness and the negative impressions

124

brought from the working environment. This is a wave: mind to heart and heart to mind.

When we sit silently with the purpose of knowing our true selves, we experience the depth of our being.

So many things happen beyond our calculation, beyond our imagination and prediction. Every moment is fresh. Every moment is new. Every sequence is new. We may predict events vaguely, but we are not able to do so with precision. From a socio-economic point of view, one may say one is independent and self-reliant, but from a wider perspective nobody is absolutely independent. Everybody is interdependent, interrelated and spiritually connected, as we are all part of a collective consciousness.

The moment we internalize our minds and other outgoing senses, differences gradually disappear. We see things very clearly when we cross the boundary of the mind. We see little difference between others and ourselves, because we are seeing with our inner eye. When we close our physical eyes, the inner eye opens up.

While we are mostly engaged in noisy daily activities, it is hard for us to find peace and inner joy because our existence is externalized. During that period we barely feel our creative hearts. When we ask something of the heart in a rush, it will not respond instantaneously. The faculty of intuition in the heart can send whispers of guidance to the mind, but guidance must be sought in silence, allowing the heart to blossom.

22

The Experience of Consciousness

Reaching inner consciousness

Experience of our inner consciousness means experience of our presence, experience of our being and experience of our wholeness. Although we are aware of our physical and psychological existence, we often fail to experience the wholeness of being, because we are attuned to outer nature and the universe. As we project more of our resources and consciousness towards understanding and experiencing something outside of our being, we become less aware of our feeling hearts and our inner consciousness.

Discovering the inner self means discovering something outside of us that is in one way or another connected with our inner self. Anything we imagine is not just personal imagination but it is our inner reality. We are only able to imagine when there is a connection in nature with the object of imagination. If something exists in nature, it can be imagined. We are the essence of nature, the universe and the cosmos.

One day we will surely encounter extra-terrestrial beings, in the same galactic universe, and we will be baffled by their features and characteristics, far different from what we imagine. Whether we remain on earth or travel to distant galaxies, we are cosmic beings. We are connected to the entire cosmos.

Based on our earthly existence we imagine that there are beings elsewhere in the universe. Belief in life beyond earth becomes a future reality. It is not that we are less advanced and they are more advanced, since each civilization, regardless of its habitat in the cosmos, is likely to have its own unique culture and communication system. We use gestures, vocal chords and our senses to communicate, whereas aliens may have more refined methods and skills of mystical communication. Indeed, physically they may be totally different from us. So far, today's science has not been able to establish the presence of our counterparts in other galaxies. Future science will evolve further and may merge into mysticism. The term science may become obsolete and a new term coined and used. By then we will have broadened the horizons of human potential and will not recognize ourselves as we are today but as something else, more closely connected to the concept of cosmic beings. We can see a future where we may become more intuitive beings, silently communicating our thoughts.

In the deepest sense, communication means transferring the energy of information from one source of being to another. When we actually do encounter aliens, we may regret having relied only on physical communication. We may have lost the knowledge of how to use our mental energies to communicate, unlike ancient yogis, Sufis, sages and other mystics. At some point in the future, mystics, physicists and cosmologists are likely to be working together to master alternative means of communication. Then meditation will be necessary for everyone.

Relatively and regionally, we may consider ourselves to be alien. We may also consider others to be alien, but, in truth, we are always connected to everything we see and imagine because we are part of the essence of creation. This is one of the reasons why we are so inquisitive about nature and space. We are connected to them and we believe that there is something out there to pursue, understand and experience. Thus we spend most of our energy and resources doing research. This is humanity's ongoing endeavour, an enterprise of collective human consciousness.

The evolution of nature accommodates human endeavour. Whatever one's experience of nature, there is always room for disappointment or dissatisfaction with the external journey. This is a time-bound limitation. We can learn only a little during the course of our lives. We cannot even master one specific subject with complete confidence. A case in point would be the study of atoms, of human cells, of microbes such as bacteria and viruses, which has developed over centuries, occupying many scientists, yet we still do not have complete knowledge of these entities. How many more centuries will it take us to understand this subject fully and where is the time to investigate all the other entities that may exist?

Collectively we are making unceasing progress, yet we are encountering more questions, and more problems, than we faced previously. If we can combine spiritual truths and the vision of spiritually evolved people with our disciplined scientific study, we will be able to penetrate the truths of the universe much faster. Nature has infinite wisdom. A few decades ago we had only a handful of subjects to study. Now, as we advance in research, knowledge is constantly growing and will continue to do so.

The surprises and wonders in nature are inexhaustible. A single brain cannot accomplish everything in life, despite the desire to do so. Why is there such a strong wish within to see, to understand, to embrace and to experience? That impulse is not the property of our minds but comes from the depths of our hearts, because we ourselves are infinite. We have always been and we will always be infinite. And it is this infinitude that inspires powerful desires.

If our nature and consciousness were not infinite, we would not have the wish in our hearts to grow and attain the unattainable. Certain physical laws, like gravity, bind our physical bodies. There is profound meaning in being bound by these earthly laws. If we were not affected by the gravity of the earth, we could have flown away to the farthest regions of the universe. It seems that the will of nature is different from what we assume. It may be the desire of nature that we reach the unreachable only through an adventurous mystical process.

When we cease all our voluntary physical actions and stay silent, we can feel something filling up within us. Our outgoing energies are redirected to their source, to the very centre of our being. This is the mystical experience of meditation. Each time we engage in spiritual practice, we emerge with something special, something new. We look different because we have turned our thinking and perception towards the very basis of our existence. This is a deeply personal experience. Although we all share the same planet and our physical bodies are similar to one another, each of us lives at a different level according to the evolution of our inner consciousness.

Love is like light. It may be ours yet others around us will also benefit from it. We cannot say that it is ours and that we will decide whom it is to benefit. If we deliberately focus on someone upon whom to shed the light of our love, that person may feel its benefit, but the experience of the light of love in others is not within our control. For example, we can hold a flower in our hands, but we cannot easily capture its fragrance. Similarly, awakened love creates a positive effect around us. People are positively affected. Some discover their own hearts; some feel a curative effect, some find inspiration; and some find their reflection in that person's personality. Some find answers without openly questioning. These things, which happen beyond analysis and logic, we call miracles.

Feeling our inner selves at a deeper level means feeling many things outside ourselves. As our inner consciousness deepens, our perception and understanding broaden and we undergo a variety of uplifting experiences. Sometimes joy emanates from our hearts, although nobody has given us good news. We feel like dancing, singing, writing a poem, drawing or painting. We may cry tears of ecstasy. Those who do not know us may laugh at our attitude and behaviour, but we are in an ecstatic state of consciousness (*Ananda*). We submit our minds to our hearts. We surrender our hearts to our inner selves. We experience profound tenderness, flowing love and the expansion of our consciousness.

The power of touch

Touching certain key points on the body with our hands can take us to different states of consciousness. Touch can revitalize us and magnetically draw energies to the surface from the recesses of the body. If we touch without guidance from our mind and will, we cannot feel the depth of the touch, but touching with a meditative mind has a positive effect on the body and being. The emission of energy during that moment can heal aches and pains.

If we touch certain key points or energy stations in the body, beginning at the feet and finishing at the crown of the head, we feel harmony, oneness and unity. This is really a heartfelt touch that enhances beauty and energy fields and gives warmth to the body. Nothing is more comforting, beneficial and effective than our own touch.

Touching one's body and raising consciousness to the surface is a forgotten mystic art. Once we reach the crown of the head, we can bring our hands back to a restful position on the thighs. Now we can silently re-awaken the same experience within us. In this act, the mind is internally occupied and thus becomes our obedient servant. We achieve a state of peacefulness and composure. If this is pursued, it leads us to many other experiences. A genuine and determined search leads one to contentment, satisfaction, realization and enlightenment.

IX

SPACE

Feeling space means feeling the freedom of our spirit

23

Visibility and Invisibility

The experience of space

All that is visible may have emerged from the invisible.

In the cosmic cycle, every entity will eventually become invisible and timeless; and then again become visible and time-bound. Invisibility is the basis of visibility. All visible materials are held together by invisible forces, underlying forces in all matter, which can either attract or repel, as physics can explain. If we keep breaking a mountain into smaller and smaller pieces and then further into atomic particles, eventually we end up in some kind of space or nothingness; in other words the invisibility of the force that we see operating in materials. These forces of nature keep interchanging as attraction and repulsion. This interchangeability is the principal nature of the universe. Hence life is always changing and therein lies its interest. Space is the mother of all things seen and unseen and, in her womb, everything that we see today once existed in an invisible form.

Space is both conscious and unconscious; hence it gives birth to various conscious and unconscious entities. Within space there are myriad tangible objects and beings. Though we see objects and beings everywhere, in many forms, there is still room for creation in space. Whether we delve into the microscopic world or leap into the deeper macrocosmic universe, there is infinite space. There is a tendency in every human being to look into deeper space to study celestial bodies rather than only to explore the earth. Within an atom there is space between the nucleus and the orbiting electrons. Even though particles seem to touch as they bombard each other, space is maintained between them.

The concept of space is beyond mathematics. When we reach higher mathematics, we tend to become philosophical in our study and understanding. As we probe into mathematical details of the universe we become lost in our efforts to quantify it.

All objects that are visible in nature have a boundary. Thus, every entity retains its uniqueness and individuality. But human consciousness has no boundary.

Unlimited consciousness dwells in the limited physical body – this is the cosmic adventure of higher consciousness. When we descend into the inner universe, we come very close to the unlimited experience of space. Thus we have a tendency to close our eyes when we want to experience the conscious presence in the body. When we direct externalized consciousness into the inner being, we experience space in its vastness. This is a true experience of space. Our consciousness soars higher and higher, transcending all the limits of the tangible universe.

The experience one gains internally cannot be explained in mere neurological or biological terms. Many western scientists (though by no means all) prefer to regard all emotional and spiritual experiences as residing solely in the brain and to have a purely physiological origin. The beauty of creation is that physical analysis has a physical source, while the metaphysical experience has a non-physical source. The closest analogy to the invisible spiritual heart is the physical heart. The spiritual heart cannot be accessed by our mind but by our will and volition, in which very little thinking is involved and more feeling prevails. Both the mind and the spiritual heart are composed of the same consciousness but in different states: the former is exciting, the latter is fulfilling. Spiritual experience is a personal experience. Anyone who wants to prove or disprove another person's experience of consciousness or space can have only a limited understanding of the outline of that person's being. Everybody has their own unique individual standpoint of perception, according to the level of evolution of their consciousness.

Space can be perceived or experienced in the human brain only if there is the ability to perceive it esoterically. *The space in the human brain is mystical* and is on a different scale from the scale we usually apply to measure the space outside ourselves. The rational brain alone, without the help of heart and consciousness, does not have an overall view and experience of an object.

Expansion of consciousness also means an experience of limitless space. Consciousness expands as we gain more experience of space, because space contains everything. When that space is experienced in all that surrounds us, we begin to feel oneness with the environment, with other people and with the universe. In order to experience universal oneness, we have to have a big heart to forgive people who cause trouble and to embrace everyone as part of our existence. We experience oneness with them. We embrace everyone in our consciousness with acceptance and compassion. This state of consciousness has transformational energy. When we reject someone, they reject us; if we try controlling others, our feeling of insecurity increases and none of us progress. There may be many temporary solutions for every problem but there is only one solution that is long lasting, and that is to raise spiritual awareness.

If people have embraced us in their consciousness, we feel it when we are around them. They identify their relationship with us intuitively. If they have *not* welcomed us in their consciousness, even if we live close to them, we feel distant.

The visible manifestation of cosmic consciousness is the universe within which we exist. We explore the universe on a range of scales, from our planet to galaxies, through disciplined study, which is a scientific approach. Similarly, we explore invisible consciousness and forces in nature by means of love, which is a spiritual approach. Fulfilment occurs in our lives when we approach both equally.

We cannot meditate all the time, asserting that we are spiritual and evolving spiritually. If that were the whole purpose of the universe, then the vast majority of people in the world would not have been tempted to explore and change it. On the other hand, if materialism were everything, then no one would have had the urge to search for truth and peace. Most of us feel the need to do both, which implies that, when material and spiritual life complement each other, we become more evolved and fulfilled.

Some may say that they achieve fulfilment in life only through material gain and others say fulfilment in life can be achieved only by living in a more spiritual way. In each case, something remains unexperienced and unfulfilled in the totality of life. Eventually, for everyone, a spiritual way of thinking and living becomes the foundation for life. In the meantime, it is an individual's choice whether to project their energy, resources and consciousness towards full-scale material living, to devote their life entirely to spiritual enlightenment, or to create an adventurous balance between the two.

Accountability is the essence of a true human being.

The combination of these two approaches is possible, but we are always pulled to one side or the other. The extent of this pull depends on one's background, mentality or individual choice. Not all of us can become vegetarians and not all of us in the world are omnivores. Although each of us has an innate tendency to look for peace and enlightenment, not all of us will do so. This is the nature of the world. But we cannot blame the world and attribute our mistakes or follies to nature. It is important to take responsibility for our growth or decline. We cannot escape our consciences.

Regardless of our choices, somewhere, at some point, we all come to search for peace and the realization of the deeper self. This becomes possible when we withdraw ourselves from the chaotic, tempting world and walk into silence. Then a meditative consciousness is experienced effortlessly. We discover more of ourselves during silence, as we are in a space where we are less influenced by the world. Sometimes the experience of inner space becomes a spontaneous mystical experience. Spiritual insight provides many physical and psychological benefits, but these are only peripheral to attaining enlightenment.

Timeless consciousness and limitless space interact eternally, creating time, energy, matter and the manifestation of living entities. Energy is only another form of matter.

We are both energy and matter. We have time-bound bodies and timeless consciousness.

Our deeper selves and our bodies contain all the codes, formulae, equations and secrets of the universe. Thus human curiosity is unending. We are everything. We are sometimes destructive and sometimes constructive, but we have the innate wish to experience timeless consciousness and limitless space within.

The attempt to explore and experience the inner side of one's existence is both spiritual and mystical. Achieving peace, finding answers, realizing the true self, and establishing the connection between one's self and the higher Self, are all various touchstones on the journey of enlightenment.

The whole process reflects a leap from ordinary thinking to greater understanding, a journey from intellect to intuition, from the externalized mind to inner consciousness. Expanding our consciousness means deepening our feelings, emotions and awareness. Doubts, disbelief and questions wither away with the rise of clarity, realization and the wisdom of the spiritual sun.

24

Awareness of Inner Space

Some people travel to a holy place to find a reflection or reminder of their holy inner space. When they are there, they become revived and recharged; some gain deeper mystical insights and have richer spiritual experiences, while others find direction. Centres of pilgrimage are kept separate from worldly activity. Pilgrims are attracted to them because of their positive influence, so they bring only positive thoughts and, through collective consciousness, they contribute only positive energies to these holy places. Yet nothing is as holy as our inner space.

We should think of the entire planet as a holy place, yet we do not do so. While only a few places on earth are defined as holy, some exceptional people who have advanced spiritually, and have heightened their consciousness with constant inner awareness, perceive everything as holy.

Unless one's inner space is deeply felt and embraced, one cannot intuit the holiness of the universe and of every being.

When a baby is born, he or she looks fresh and appealing because the inner space in the child's body is like an undisturbed lake spreading out to the horizon. There is no trace of negativity in newborn babies as no external information has yet entered their space. Logic, reasoning and common sense do not exist in newborns; simplicity and innocence prevail. Everything is perfect: a baby's smile can light up our hearts and even a child's screams can have a certain melody. Since babies are holy, their inner space is pure, without the fog of impressions and information that reduces mystical inner space.

Every day new information enters the consciousness of a child, leading the parents to feel proud of their baby's growth and learning. In this process, inner space becomes cluttered with myriad disturbing images and the debris of excess information. Gradually, the mind structures itself in rational thought through a faculty called intellect, which prevails in the head. As a consequence, the possibility of retaining a peaceful state of consciousness and the purity of inner space becomes remote.

As children progress on their journey through life, we witness many physical, psychological and emotional changes, proportional to the information gathered, and the impressions of experiences are imprinted on their bodies and minds. The child's appearance, demeanour, attitude and vibrations reflect what has been absorbed from the world in the course of the journey, in the process of growth. If our home becomes cluttered, we can tidy it up, renovate it, and work to convert it into a pleasant, habitable place. The solution to such untidiness is straightforward, although it may take time. Similarly, if inner space is filled with unpleasant and unwanted information and impressions, it takes time to remove these imprints of negativity. In our inner space others cannot help us. We must work within ourselves, breathing out what is unimportant and retaining what is essential.

We can find help through meditation. Spiritual inspiration comes to us when our hearts are receptive and helps us overcome the influence of deep-seated, inessential information. We live deep within the chambers of our hearts, even though the extension of our inner consciousness appears in the head, on the surface of our physical existence. At our will and wish, we can project ourselves onto the surface or we can recede into the sacred sanctuary of our hearts. As we float on the surface of existence, we have to defend ourselves frequently. There are multiple forces invading our consciousness; so many things obstruct our way, and we have no control over them.

Just as we exist in our present state, other entities have their own existence, tasks and nature. If light has a positive nature, darkness has its own negativity. Every entity is equipped with protective instincts and defensive skills. We cannot break a rock by touching it softly or by using words. Even if we use an implement, we still have to overcome the rock's resistance. The rock exercises this resistance in its own way, to protect its existence, its nature and its properties. Similarly, all human and non-human species exercise unique defensive abilities when threatened. If we attempt to touch an ant, even gently, it runs away from us. Every being resists or guards itself to the degree necessary to repel the danger posed by invaders. Human beings, however, have an extra defensive resource, which is rational intelligence.

A single stimulus is enough to generate a sensation of fear, trigger deep-seated, negative memories or alter our mood. It can effect many changes within us, either positive or negative. It is through our eyes and other senses that information is accessed and outside forces invade. Thus, there is an innate tendency in all human beings to close their eyes when there is extreme danger or when something beautiful or inspiring occurs before them. By closing our eyes upon seeing something unpleasant or disturbing, we block negative forces entering our consciousness and we give out positive defensive vibrations in an unconscious meditative state. We embrace ourselves and exclude the external incident. Conversely, when we close our eyes upon seeing something extraordinarily beautiful, we absorb the essence of what we are witnessing and connect the Self to outer beauty while in a meditative state. Thus we embrace that *beauty* with our consciousness.

Sometimes, when our hearts feel the need to experience silence, our eyes close spontaneously. There is something happening inside us: perhaps guidance is coming to us from within or someone may be communicating with us on a mystical or spiritual level. Our essential being may be forewarned of events that may occur either close by or more distantly. Perhaps we are being guided towards a spontaneous meditation (*Dhyana*) or keeping in touch with our own unique purpose, meaning and the conscious evolution of our being. If this is the case, we should immediately engage in intuitive, meditative silence.

It is not how long we meditate, but how effective our meditation is that matters.

Some people force themselves to meditate, which is not beneficial. We do not have to meditate all the time, avoiding life's other duties. We can raise our awareness of our need for meditation. Sitting or otherwise positioning the body in a comfortable manner and keeping the eyes shut keeps us in touch with our essential inner being, the Self. There are no time constraints; it is we who decide how long genuine meditation will last in our hearts and in our deeper consciousness. It is not how long we meditate, but how effective our meditation is that matters. We should note that meditation also reflects on the material world in a unique manner, though not always according to the standards set by society. We may not gain more wealth, success and reward in terms of social criteria, but we can experience miracles in the form of uplifting events.

As we progress on our inner spiritual journey, we discover that we are not separate from others. In different proportions, we are part of everything, everyone and every occurrence. As our consciousness evolves, we discover our ability to create an auric field that extends like a shield around us. Through this, we communicate with nature and the universe. We also gain the ability to cancel out some of the destructive energy coming from outside forces, or at least to reduce its impact. These metaphysical activities take place unconsciously but their positive effects are registered in our consciousness.

Some people approach meditation like an instant medication. They keep their eyes closed and sit for a while, then give up, saying they cannot meditate, because shifting thoughts are constantly disturbing their equilibrium. Such people expect to change instantaneously from one state of consciousness to another and to be dipped into an ocean of peace. If we really want to meditate, we have to learn the nature of the many components of our existence, from the mind to our senses to the whole body. Before we enter meditation, we have to experience these entities individually. This is an act of purification in preparation for the main meditation. We cannot stop the river of the mind all of a sudden, causing it to overflow and flood.

Instead, we have to direct the river to flow in a particular direction. The military use force, politicians use power and poets use words, but spiritually developed people use their thoughts, and then act with conscious awareness.

We can apply all of these practices, using our discretion. Sometimes we need to force ourselves to exercise until we develop disciplined habits. Sometimes we have to use words to convey our meaning. And sometimes we must deepen our thoughts so as to translate powerful curative and inspirational beams of energy into physical reality. We unfold ourselves through silence by meditating, a process that is not entirely conscious. The successful achievement of a meditative state is a celebration.

Since, over the passage of centuries, we have made the mind our main tool, it requires dedication, effort and time to overcome this influence and to yield instead to the inner voice of the heart. We must let thoughts pass by; we must try to ignore images that tease us; we must let go of disturbing memories of the past. We must be patient and say to ourselves that we are attracted to material things but not attached to them. We may be critical in our views and comments about others and the world but must not be hateful.

Before we enter the inner realms of peace, we must bypass the mind's obstructions. As soon as we close our eyes in meditation, the mind obstructs us. If we accept this about the mind, then we can even enjoy its disturbing nature en route to the peaceful heart, and thence to the deep, silent sea of consciousness. In this separate world of ours, the universe exists in a higher dimension, which in turn can lead us to deeper spiritual experience. The whole process of experiencing inner space is a Self-discovery.

By expanding consciousness, we expand our inner space and we become enlightened cosmic beings, not merely human beings.

We have vision beyond the power of physical sight and hear melody beyond the range of human hearing. We become a source of inspiration for many. We unfold all that is within us. We have no expectations or anticipation. We subdue our egotistic minds and re-experience innocence. It is in innocence that all kinds of beautiful experiences occur; it is in innocence that inner space is felt deeply and experienced wholly.

25

Inner and Outer Space

When we are alive, we have consciousness. When we die we merge into the universal consciousness and obey the laws of the evolutionary principles of universal nature, unless we make an individual spiritual endeavour to retain our individual conscious awareness. We may do this to journey either back onto the earth plane, into other dimensions in the universe or deliberately to merge with the universal consciousness of creation. Fortunately, we are blessed with so much freedom and compassion in our will, consciousness, feelings and thinking, that with these abilities we can guide and lead our lives in whichever direction or dimension we wish to journey, and translate our wishes into greater realities.

A magnet is physical. Magnetism is an experience of the non-physical in the physical. The magnetism that scientists understand is physical but the magnetic attraction experienced within us and in others is a mystical experience. 'Magnetism' is a quality that attracts others. One becomes more magnetic when one realizes the spiritual Self within. Realization of the Self within is one aspect of being; experiencing the Self is another. These two aspects constitute a whole experience of being in the past, being in the present and being in the future. An experiment is physical. The experience of the experiment is personal, or metaphysical. Matter is physical, whereas energy in the broader sense can only be experienced indirectly, via the physical. The human body is tangible, so it is corporeal. Human consciousness is partly physical and partly mystical, leading one to deeper spiritual experiences. Consciousness is at the core of all creation. From microbes to elephants and whales, there is consciousness. In plants and trees we find a different implementation of the laws of nature, which we can also describe as consciousness. From particles like quarks to the grandeur of Mount Everest, the same laws of nature apply, so we can say that there is consciousness, the pulsation of consciousness and the vibration of the same conscious force everywhere.

Inanimate objects are unconscious of their consciousness, i.e. they obey the laws of nature without any awareness of them. All conscious entities, however, are aware and conscious of their existence. Humans are greatly conscious of their consciousness. There is consciousness throughout space and time, but the levels of consciousness vary. Creation and dissolution are nothing but the pulsation of universal consciousness, or super-consciousness; they are like the day and night of higher nature.

Creation and dissolution are sometimes local and sometimes non-local in space. There cannot be absolute dissolution in creation. There is always function, vibration and movement. Stillness is impossible in the universe. No elementary particle has been found that does not have vibrational energy. There is always vibration; there is always a wave-like motion. There is an observable outer difference between objects, between conscious entities that exist in a microcosm or a macrocosm, yet with our consciousness we can connect with any other conscious entity.

148

As we journey deeper and deeper into matter and energy, we become lost in a kind of space. Though atoms are unbelievably small, there is a vast space between the nuclei of atoms and their periphery. If we investigate consciousness even further, we find only space. When we look up at the sky during the night, we see stars sparsely scattered in space, though each star is incalculably large. Similarly, though the human brain is so small, even when compared to the size of the human body, it can receive, process and reciprocate an abundance of information and an infinite number of images, because it has 'storage space' within its network.

There is no analogy to consciousness. It stands alone, beautiful and unparalleled. The best way we can envisage consciousness is as a form of space.

The planet earth is rotating and orbiting because it obeys the laws of nature stored deep within its consciousness, from universal consciousness. This is the power of oneness. Thus, there is a tendency in every human being to be especially conscious of space. If we do not have our own space, we feel oppressed. We need space to stretch the body and the mind. We need space to express our emotions and to expand our consciousness. Sometimes space is comprehended as consciousness and vice versa.

When we see a rich expanse of fields, we immediately feel a sense of elation and freedom of spirit. No matter how preoccupied we are or how busy with social commitments and responsibilities, something uplifting happens. We cannot adequately express our feelings about this experience. We are moved because consciousness outside us reflects within us and for a moment we become one with it. We are reminded of our individual existence in physical form and surrounded by a mental boundary of 'I-ness' or ego.

Many scientists, interested in astronomy, wish to journey to the planets to gain greater knowledge. When astronauts return to earth, their perceptions have usually changed dramatically. Many astronauts have written of their experiences in space after observing the planets and viewing the earth from a different perspective.

If we live in a pleasant environment, for example in the countryside, where there is space for each person to develop, we tend to find that people are generally more warm-hearted than the people who live in cities, where everyone is too close together. The moment we greet people in a pleasant environment we are likely to receive a friendly and eager response. If we ask for something, they will rarely refuse us. This is because of the effect of expansive space. In a complementary way, if we want to discover the inner universe, we have to go into solitary contemplation. We have to sit in a cave or a hut or a cosy house in order to fathom the deeper self. If we want to experience the outer consciousness of creation, we have to emerge from isolation, breaking through all physical limits and mental confines to think and feel beyond horizons.

If we want both the inner and outer universes, we have to accept solitude and universality. The process of shifting consciousness from understanding to experiencing consciousness is metaphysical, encompassing all the subjects that lead to a higher understanding and experience of beauty, love and truth. The mind and body can be thought of as wings that allow us to glide through our inner space.

No one can establish either scepticism or theism, i.e. the existence or non-existence of God, by the use of logic alone. Consistent denial may lead to the core of our inner spiritual truth but the realization of scepticism is dry. Sometimes it may bring clarity but not fulfilment. Truth comprehended from mere rationality should lead us to enter the realms of deeper truths within ourselves but should not result in confusion and scepticism about our own potential and capabilities. There are truths that exist beyond our rational minds and these can be experienced through silent personal endeavour, which is spiritual. Both facets of the truth, be they objective or subjective, become illumined within our hearts and spirits.

All kinds of questions are encouraged in secular sciences. Indeed, questioning is the way to learn. Children are taught from a very young age to ask questions. When children return home from school, and are asked to do some simple task, they immediately ask why. If asked to smile, they ask why. Asked to cry, they still ask why. Asked not to ask any questions because we are going to say something to them, they still ask why. Questioning enables us to gain physical knowledge. However, after a time, we wish to learn something intuitive by using our emotional awareness. To do this, we must prepare ourselves by means of silence. There are no questions, only inquiry, because we are not asking anyone else. We inquire internally: who am I, what is my true nature? Where do I come from, what is my destination and purpose, how am I connected to nature, how am I related to the universe, what is my uniqueness and what is my maximum potential? How can I explore and experience my

151

realization and how can I help serve or assist others to achieve greater fulfilment? Certainly not everyone will find answers to all these questions, but some responses will be found during the process of deeper inquiry through silence or meditation. These may then provide the key to other answers.

Silence begins when we stop asking questions about the science of our being. When we withdraw our consciousness from the region of our head to the heart, we have entered the silence of our inner consciousness and inner Being. To do so, we should adopt a posture that is comfortable for us.

We all close our eyes when we sleep. When affected by dust, we close our eyes. If our eyes are sore, we close them. When we close our eyes, with the sincere purpose of experiencing our body, mind, heart, and deeper than that, then different manifestations of inner consciousness will arise. We will be graced with a mystical experience. All the different layers of existence are unfurled. Our experience is the testimony.

The words 'I believe' can encompass or embrace so much. We can achieve personal spiritual growth. At the same time we can be helpful to others. Our very presence is an inspiration to those who surround us. We begin to see our reflection in everything and everyone.

When we meet spiritually developed people, the experience reflects and reconfirms that we are journeying into our inner dimensions of consciousness. If we are open to them and sometimes even if we are not, after every encounter with such individuals, after every conversation with the spiritually evolved, we experience many changes within us and find so much improvement in our lives.

Spiritual expansion means the expansion of consciousness. It means exploring all that we possess within us. In an expanded state of consciousness fear disappears, confusion dissolves and clarity dawns. We are conscious of thoughts, words and deeds and their effects. As a result, we can create any type of impression on our consciousness that we desire.

X

TIME

Time affects all that is visible but not the invisible spirits of our being

26

The Three Folds of the Day

The three folds of the day are symbolic of our states of consciousness and of what we express. Morning is physical, afternoon is mystical and evening is spiritual. The effect of speaking aloud indicates a morning mood. Speaking in whispers is indicative of the sun being at the meridian. Speaking softly reflects an evening mood.

Morning

Morning is driving, motivational, tempting, worldly, physical and sometimes chaotic. During the morning, consciousness manifests itself more in the head. Our minds become hungry for new information, seeking excitement and stimulating new ideas for survival. We put the past behind us, accept the present and look forward to facing the future.

Just before sunrise, the mind is fresh, more receptive, and very close to the heart, so this is a perfect time for meditation or contemplation of important issues. Partly because there is less carbon dioxide being produced by human activity, before dawn there is an abundance of oxygen and positive energy in the environment that surrounds us. Externally, the world is mostly silent and less disturbed by thought vibrations, and our bodies are well rested, making morning meditation effective and uplifting. In the context of early morning meditation, the influx of local thoughts is low, almost negligible, having little effect on the minds of those meditating.

What about the thoughts coming from people on the other side of the world? Like radio waves, thoughts can penetrate the atmosphere and traverse great distances searching for the intended object, provided that they are powered by our spirits. For this to happen, consciousness must descend from the head to the core-being.

When we awake, information comes from every direction, from radios, newspapers, magazines, television and the internet. We are bombarded with thought waves from all directions. Our brain is exposed to the numerous intense stimuli generated by a chaotic world.

A single negative piece of information or negative thought is enough to disturb the entire day. The sense of negativity remains throughout the day. Ripples of images are generated in the lakes of our minds, stirring the underlying negative impressions that in turn affect our bodies, our words, our vibrations and others around us. This negativity may also spoil the following day. Sometimes the negative effects exist for a long period of time. No matter how we try to avoid these effects, the cleansing process does not occur instantaneously: the process begins by creating an evening atmosphere within us. We need inspiration as a spiritual gift to gain greater understanding of our actions, thoughts, movements and their consequences.

Afternoon

Afternoon or mid-day is somewhat mystical in nature, as it is neither too physical nor deeply spiritual. When the sky is clear and the sun's rays fall directly on our heads, they stimulate the pineal gland and the unexplored areas of the brain, which enhances the power of reception, retention and imagination. In the past some scholars and yogis either shaved their heads completely or kept their hair short, in order to maximize the benefits of the sun's stimulation of the areas of the brain. Thus, afternoon is also a beneficial time for meditation, since body, mind and spirit, and the sun and earth, are all aligned with time, space and consciousness.

Most of us focus primarily on physical fitness rather than on the benefits to be derived from meditation, which should be a foremost priority and should be the foundation of the day's agenda. As most of us have not yet realized this truth, there is a dearth of peace and harmony in today's world. The positive contributions of a few individuals are not enough to resolve impending problems; each of us needs to accept responsibility for our planet, the environment, nature and our collective well-being.

Evening

In the morning, consciousness dwells mostly in the mind and less in the heart. In the evening, the opposite circumstances prevail.

Evening evokes feelings of serenity, especially when we are surrounded by nature. Evening mellows hardened minds, creates greater tenderness and the feeling of being soothed. In the evening, just before sunset, the crime rate is often low. Though things may change in the course of the night, at dusk the world is calm. At this time, regardless of how many problems and irritations we have, solace can be found. We are less worried. The world's effect on our being is lessened. It is a time for withdrawal. It is also a good time to reflect on the day just past and to make decisions for the next.

Evening is a treasured part of the day, ripe in possibility. It is serene. The night is considered the morning by people who are looking for pleasure or entertainment. As the evening progresses, we experience a longing for the surroundings of home. As the sun goes down in the west, stars begin to appear, with their many messages for observers.

In the evening our minds swing gently from wakefulness to a state of somnolence or to a peaceful sleep, from which we are taken to the world of dreams. As evening sets in, we seek peace within ourselves, the companionship of our loved ones and the tranquillity of home. The process of cleansing ourselves begins by creating an evening atmosphere. If we have peace and serenity within us, we have achieved most of our goals of the day. Some people are of the opinion that peace is only experienced after the fulfilment of personal goals.

We can compare the reactions of others as we greet them at various times of day.

At noon we are between morning and evening. We are neither spiritual nor materialist. We do not know what is actually important for us. In that fleeting moment, we experience rays of sunlight shining directly on our heads. Even if we are out of the sun, the influence of these rays cannot be avoided. Though reduced, the effect is still present.

In the morning, then at noon, and again in the evening, we witness a rotation of the mind. The response to our greetings will be the most peaceful in the evening. The experience of evening's tranquillity renews us for the next day. Thus life will appear interesting and curious: there is always something new to come.

From evening to the next morning, many changes occur in the body. Millions of cells are born and discarded by the body's built-in mechanical systems. Energy is circulated in many ways, in many forms, at different levels within the body, until it is reconstituted as mental energy. If we do not convert this energy into conscious positive energy, there is nothing to look forward to in life. We are engulfed in sameness and lack motivation. We find nothing to celebrate. However, some rare songs and films, and certain gifts that we receive, have inspirational qualities. No matter how often we hear, see or handle them, we are never bored. A gift that has sentimental value enables us to renew and recreate the mood of sweet moments. It always radiates energy, reminding us of our connection with a person or with a time when we were emotionally moved. Alternatively, that source of inspiration may awaken sentiments that take us away from our current discomforts.

Age and youth

From a cosmic point of view, there is nothing old or new in the universe. The sense of time is realized only from individual perspectives. Something 'old' is what has been experienced, embraced and seen; something 'new' is yet to be experienced, to be received. People who grow old are new to people who are just coming into the world. Grandparents are much loved by their grandchildren. From the child's perspective, grandparents are not old. Grandchildren form a new friendship, possibly a better friendship, with their grandparents than with their parents or friends. Hence, we see much closeness between grandparents and grandchildren. From the grandchild's perspective, grandparents are young and possess the same spirit as they do.

There are trees that are more than a thousand years old. Old trees are very strong, stronger than young trees because their roots are deep in the earth. They are difficult to uproot as they occupy a large area. Similarly, when people grow old, their spiritual roots deepen. They may or may not be aware of this process, but it does take place over time. Those who are aware of it become enlightened when they realize their roots, their resources and their potential, as well as the purpose and meaning of their existence.

When we are attuned to our breathing, our waves of consciousness, our beating heart and our rhythmic being, we are able to make time in the universe stand still. *Our being is our essence.* Neither age nor youth affects us. When we are engaged in friendly, sportive activities, joyous tasks that we love, when we are absorbed in meaningful silence, we feel ever-youthful and ageless.

27

The Invisible Clock

There is a veil between the past and the future, between birth and death, the mind and the heart, the physical body and the non-physical spirit. It is what makes life interesting and exhilarating. There is anticipation, incentive and motivation to live life, to know, explore and experience the truth behind and beyond the veil. We can penetrate the veil only through internalization of all that is revealed to us in existence; then we experience unity and oneness. This experience leads to raised consciousness and a brightening of the light within.

The nature of time

Time is a wheel that rotates unceasingly. It has been rotating with the earth's orbit, with the orbit of the planets and with the movement of celestial bodies. Time and space are so deeply interwoven that they cannot be separated. There is something beyond time and space, but it is very difficult to understand with our limited intellectual capacity. We need to explore our intuitive resources so that the intellect and intuition complement each other and help us achieve the seemingly impossible. Our logical minds should be at the vanguard of our exploration of the journey of life, assisting us to discover, invent, learn and experience the very truths and facts of life. However, this same mind can be a barrier to visualizing something we have never before seen or experienced. On the other hand, if we depend solely on our minds, we will miss the truth that lies beyond our sensory perception. In other words, we should also let our intuition guide us so that we can experience and explore the truth that awaits us all.

The body is finite, but the consciousness is infinite.

We divide time into three phases: past, present and future, but there is only one cosmic time. It is no wonder that there are so many stories that explore the concept of time travel to the past and the future. The present is just one perspective, a point of observation.

The past is something that has already been experienced and the future is something yet to be experienced. The present is the meeting point of the past and the future. It is also a coordinate, in the mathematical sense, of observation and a presence in the time in which we project our minds. The present is being – that is, living in the present state of awareness of what is happening around us, with or without our participation. In the present, we have only a vague vision of the future – be it about ourselves, about others or about the world at large. We do not have a definitive vision of the unfolding of future events. The renowned prophets of the past made many prophecies, in prose and poetry. Regardless of their form, these prophecies contain truths, but they are not expressed in unequivocal terms. Only pupils of that traditional school of thought can make a broad interpretation of these prophecies, reading them with intuitive hearts. We do have the power to shed light on the future with our intuitive abilities. Intuition is one of our spiritual resources and it enables us to have vision and direction, by heeding the signs of our animal existence.

Whether we are asleep or awake, we are always constrained by time. Whatever we do, be it in sorrow or in happiness, the wheel of time moves on. It can neither be stopped nor reversed. This is the fixed nature of time. It is a beam of light moving in one direction, an eternal arrow.

Our concept of time varies according to our emotional states of mind or our consciousness. If we are happy, our concept of time becomes condensed. We exclaim, 'My goodness! I had no idea I spent so many hours on this! Where did the time go?' But we cannot write off that span of time in the book of our lives nor can we re-enter that time zone in the fullest sense. The concept of time did not affect our consciousness at that point because we were in an elevated state of happiness. Our hearts blossomed; our minds receded; our bodies were absorbed in bliss, ecstasy and the fullness of love. Conversely, if we are in anguish or agony, our concept of time dilates or stretches.

We are in awe as to how time passed during a particular experience on the voyage of life. Time did not affect us in the way that it usually does when we are waiting for someone or something, or when we are experiencing a difficult period of our lives. When we are deeply absorbed, either by external nature around us or by the inner nature of our consciousness, we are able to keep the overwhelming aspect of time at bay. In that state of consciousness, we become timeless, conscious beings – it becomes a relief to go from time-bound thinking to timeless feeling. The process refreshes us, revitalizing our bodies, minds and spirits.

Time is energy. Time is life. Time is money. Time is everything. The twelve months can be likened to the twelve wheels on the chariot of time. We are set in motion in accordance with the rotation of the wheel of time. As our physical bodies are time-bound, we have no option but to follow the rhythm of time. We may slacken in our duties and activities but time will not cease. Time ticks by with the beat of our hearts, with the pulsing of our nerves, with the circulation of our blood, with the ebb and flow of our breathing and with the waves of our consciousness. Time is mystical. It is not a mechanical clock that we stare at. Although we have divided time into splinters of seconds, it is still indivisibly infinite and remains abstract beyond our conception.

If we become too calculating about our lives – if we set too many goals or become too greedy in acquiring material things, status, reputation and position – we while away our time, not able to experience life deeply. On the other hand, we cannot ignore worldly life and worldly attainments, because they are pervasive. Nevertheless, our satisfaction level rises when we have a positive attitude, when we are open in the truest sense, when we do not limit our understanding or experience of the world, internally and externally. We open up all possible doors of life so that light can enter from any direction and inspiration can flow into our beings from any source.

If we want to attain satisfaction, we have to learn how to appreciate what we have already experienced and what we already possess within us. When we appreciate what we have, we become qualified for higher gifts, attainments and greater success. But instead of appreciation, we make our lives empty. We choose discontent. It is a wonderful compliment when we truly appreciate others, telling them how attractive they look and how kind, friendly and generous they are. Sincere praise is a great spiritual and inspirational gift that we can offer. If we seal ourselves off, asking, 'Why do I have to praise others?', we stunt our growth, not only spiritually but also in many aspects of life.

Our future depends upon how we are today, what our attitude is at this time, how much endurance and breadth we have within us to accept our circumstances before we alter them. The future also depends upon our nature. We possess a wealth of resources within us. There is much for us to appreciate. We rarely look into ourselves. We spend energy lavishly in the outer world. We seem to forget that by reaching and exploring the depths of the inner world, we will have much greater success in the external world.

Even at this moment, time is ticking along with our heartbeats, along with the rhythm of our breathing, along with the movement of the earth and the vibration of our pulses. But we become timeless when we are absorbed in a deeper state of meditation. We become timeless when we are with those we truly love. We gain the experience of timelessness when we are engaged in the kind of activity that brings happiness not only to us, but to others as well. Is there any greater adventure a human being can experience than becoming timeless in the time-bound world, in the time-bound body, in a universe of cosmic time?

Emotion as experience

When we live for emotion, we bathe in surging waves of feelings. The after-effect is a feeling of freshness, greater vitality and a revival of our emotional self. This should not be interpreted to mean that we have to weep or cry to revitalize the emotional being. We have to experience both controlled and uncontrolled emotion, as both are a natural part of the emotional state. Suppressed emotion is unhealthy because it causes negative effects on the body and mind. We can subdue our egos, but not our emotions. Waves of emotions have a cleansing effect on our bodies, minds and spirits. Aristotle called this effect 'catharsis'.

Emotions are necessary for human beings to journey from cruelty to kindness and from aggression to compassion, so that we can be respectful and considerate to animals, plants and mother earth as a whole. Through emotion, we seek environmental soundness and beauty.

Suppose we receive a special gift from a loved one. We have so much love for that object that, if we were to lose it, we would experience despair. If we were to recover the gift, we would feel elated. Both kinds of emotion are natural and necessary, but positive emotions are always elevating and curative.

Apart from our physical and mental resources, nature has also blessed us with mystical abilities. When we want to convey our deeper feelings or thoughts, we use many words in an effort to make others understand us. But sometimes a mere gesture or a note of mystic silence is much more effective in expressing our intended meanings to others. Alternatively, if we say something in a whisper, the message goes straight to the heart, bypassing the constrictions of the mind.

When we say 'I love you' loudly to our favourite people, it doesn't accurately convey our meaning. When we shout, sweetness and tenderness are lost, but if we whisper the same words, they are remembered forever. We whisper not only our words, but also our warmth, breath and currents of emotional being. These imprints remain on our loved ones' consciousness for a long, long time.

The meaning of success

When viewed only from physical, social and worldly perspectives, life appears to be a web of intricacies. The journey of life is like a labyrinth with many twists and many people encountered on our journey. Psychologically or emotionally, we may sometimes feel alone, but we are not alone in the context of society and the world. Wherever we go, society follows us like a shadow. We create this web.

Life is like a game, a battle of minds. If we are aggressive, we advance, particularly if our aggression is sensible and controlled. The controlled use of aggression creates many opportunities and is a launching pad for success.

We draw rules to be followed, or changed. In the course of fulfilling the obligations of society, our freedoms become constricted. We call ourselves democrats, but most of the time we are not the lovers of our lives; on the contrary, we become the dictators of our lives and of the lives of others.

Society has a yardstick to measure whether somebody is successful or not, and that is material growth. Perhaps people who are unsuccessful in social terms have invaluable wealth in them that they need to recognize, with their smiles, good sleep, good health, friendship, consideration of others, and time to meditate, read and relax.

Why are only a few rich and successful? Others have made a different choice; they did not want to become deeply involved in the web of society. Maybe they opted to spend their time in some other ways, living life according to their own principles and wishes. This is a personal decision – a method of understanding and living life. Others may honour or dishonour us, but if we are truly happy, then that is all that matters. There are many people who are rich in the material or worldly sense, but have they been able to realize their treasures within? Are they really satisfied with their lives? These questions remain open and others cannot draw conclusions as to the answers, but rather must learn from observation or personal disclosures.

If nature is rich and we are the children of nature, how can we be poor? The answer is that we cannot be. Determination will take us to our destination – undaunted unswerving determination. If we do not have monetary resources, we can still embark upon a career. If we cannot walk, we can still find other ways of reaching a destination. If we cannot speak or even gesticulate, we can still transmit our thoughts to others. We can still make things happen. There are scientists, scholars and industrialists who have achieved much in spite of major physical disabilities or problems in their personal lives. They were able to do so through vision, determination and persuasion.

The first and most important vision is clarity.

Some people say, 'I am confused; I don't know what to do'. This means that their expectations are too great. They want to achieve too much too quickly. They do not want to compromise. Thus, they are confused. They are oscillating restless and unsettled. But, if they come to realize that we can only have

169

something and not everything at a given time, they will become settled. If desire is uncontrolled it becomes greed. With this awareness, confusion melts away.

The meaning of meditation

The first and final act we should perform before we enter into any work is meditation. We must experience the unique nature of our individual existence. We must divine a worldly purpose according to the unique nature and resources that we possess. Then we will feel contentment and satisfaction. Then we will progress. Meditation leads us to that stage.

In a broader perspective; the whole Universe is a meditational place. All the subjects we deal with in life are the subjects of meditation. We are the meditators. Every experience in life is part meditation if it is taken seriously, sincerely and consciously.

What is meditation? Meditation means becoming one with our thoughts, words and actions and becoming one with the Self where the universe is our home. Meditation is necessary before and after every task. The intensity of meditation should be proportional to the nature of the task, which must be judged individually. We have to crystallize our thoughts about what we actually want to do, because life is a sea of consciousness and opportunities. We must decide what we want. We cannot achieve everything. Some go to the ocean to drill for oil. Some go fishing. Some go on holiday. Some go for romance. Some go for meditation. Some go to find the inspiration to write poetry. Each of us has to make our own choices. Raising spiritual awareness through meditation will help us to realize the meaning of life rather than regretting the choices we made.

At the beginning of meditation, the first thought that emerges in our minds is, 'I cannot concentrate'. For decades, meditation instructors and books on meditation have implied that concentration is the goal. Mere concentration is not meditation. Concentration is just an exercise of the mind. Either let go of everything or let everything come in. If we waste our time focusing on concentrating the mind, then we tend to suffer from headaches or more stress. Concentration is not a physical act. It is one of the faculties of the mind. It happens on its own when we ease our minds in a natural way, in natural surroundings and in a serene atmosphere. When we reduce our psychological stress, emotional burdens and the rigid conditioning of the mind, only then can the ability to project and focus our minds on any intended object or subject blossom and flourish. This is true concentration. It is sensitive and subtle. We submit our minds to our hearts and experience unity within. There is no artificial or technical method that suffices to teach natural meditation. If we have the will and the patience, true meditation will occur in good time.

The question then becomes: why should we meditate before beginning a task? The answer is: to experience the virtual process of the task in our consciousness and then see how our intuition could reflect upon it and bring guidance to us. We must check the points of the particular task, we must know the process of that task and we must prepare ourselves for unexpected responses and results.

The next question is: why meditate after a task is completed? Meditation after performing a task is more important than the first meditation because success may cause us to become egotistical and we may lose the value of the success, thereby hindering or halting our personal growth. Endpoint meditation is necessary so that we can conduct an overall study of how the process of a task took place. We may fail or we may succeed in our task, but we should always finish with meditation.

Fine, intuitive meditation happens spontaneously, inspirationally or naturally at the heart level, where our senses become obedient to our inner spirits and our minds become subservient to our hearts. Everything merges into a single, beautiful, unified field of experience, known as *Dhyana*.

XI

THE HEART

Through the heart we receive many gifts

28

Natural Laws and Spiritual Advancement

No matter how much time we spend speaking to one another, there is a point at which we have to become silent. Before we switch from event to event and act to act, we take pauses of silence that can be conscious or unconscious. Consciously experienced silence is inspirational and the deepening of such silence can lead us to access intuitive wisdom.

We live under the assumption that there are fixed natural laws governing forces such as gravity. However, these laws can be seen to vary in their effects when our perspective changes. Universal forces combine and recombine at different times and stages, in different patterns, making the apparently impossible possible.

There is one supreme intelligent force, hitherto unknown, that encompasses all the forces we know today. It divides into various forces and sub-forces to govern itself and its creation. This does not happen just once or twice: it is an ever-blossoming flower of creation that will never cease or fade. Creation becomes dissolved only relatively or locally in the infinitude of space. We are all a part of its beautiful pattern. These forces have a self-guiding system that is beyond our perception. We cannot create something absolutely different from the universe we live in; to invent something of that kind would be to turn against ourselves.

When we try to extend the frontiers of science too far we come close to the brink of extinction unless we use our knowledge and inventions with consideration for humanity, the planet and the environment. Such is the discipline, authority and protective nature of the universe. However, when our curious minds are harnessed together with our far-seeing intuition, there are no boundaries or limits to what we can explore and experience in this universe. We are still far from discovering the sanctuary of the secrets of life and creation. The beauty is that we have been granted the privilege of admiring, adoring and celebrating life with health, abundance and joy. However, in the course of challenging nature through our lifestyles and creativity, we have fabricated a net of minds called society and, although our physical comfort has increased, we have created domestic, national and global problems.

We need to pause and observe moments of deep silence as part of our daily lives and not only when someone passes away. When we observe silence and look inward to reconnect with the heart, with the spiritual self, we find the intuitive guidance that comes without words but with meaning. Thus, keeping in touch with the deeper spiritual self is of huge significance in our lives.

The guides are the forces of nature themselves, so guidance emanates from within them. *Everything that offers guidance is conscious, as is everything that receives guidance.* Hence we are conscious and the universe is also conscious, but we are usually unconscious of the guidance emanating from within and of the higher guidance coming into our hearts and spirits from the universe. In other words, everything is conscious in the ocean of infinite cosmic consciousness. Why are we not always conscious of this fact, when we could use it to raise our lives to the peaks of beauty, truth, love, perfect health and eternity? This is because the universe itself has a purpose and meaning that we do not yet know. We make our own assumptions and interpretations, influenced mainly by our culture, background and other circumstances since birth. We must endeavour, from the heart, to minimize the effects and limits of such imposed conditions. We have a thinking mind, which is subject to temptations and is distracted by having to respond to the information constantly entering it. Above all, we are bound by the universal laws of discipline, in order for us to exist and experience life in our physical form. Much of our energy and time is consumed by the mind in responding to and processing the information. Hence, it is not always possible to become conscious of the guidance emanating from within us and the guidance coming from the universe, unless we undertake a humble, adventurous journey. Then we will be able to have a glimpse of what the universe is for us and what we are for the universe.

In relation to our physical existence the first conscious being is the earth; then there are animals, microbes and plant species. Because we have senses, we are sensorily conscious, whereas the earth possesses greatly expressed consciousness that manifests itself as valleys, volcanoes, deserts, oases and forests. Elements, which we can think of as, for example, fire, air, water, earth and ether, are greatly conscious of their nature and are guided by higher forces to retain their specific natures and to act accordingly. These elements obey the 'laws of nature'.

The laws of the outer world are different from the laws of the inner world. In the laws of the outer world, what we say is more important than what we think and how we feel. When we are in the inner world and our consciousness is largely internalized in the heart, we think differently and what others *intend* is more important than what they say to us. In the material world, nothing is ever enough, whereas in the inner world it is contentment and quality of life that matter, rather than the accumulation of material possessions. It is when we are more present in our minds that we seek material things in the world outside.

The effect of becoming more worldly is that we become more externalized. We engage ourselves heavily in worldly activities and our existence within shrinks dramatically compared with the more obvious outer existence. As a result we become exhausted. Though we see our reflection in the mirror, we find it difficult to recognize ourselves because we have extended our minds to reach the mirage-like outside world and in the process have become outsiders to ourselves.

If someone caresses us we find it difficult to feel it because we have become outsiders to ourselves during that state of externalization. If someone shakes our hands, we do not feel their warmth; when someone hugs us, we are not there. We accept these acts of warmth and tenderness mechanically but we feel emptiness within us, because we have moved away from being in our feeling hearts.

When our being is externalized, we have less contentment and more contention; less concordance and more contradiction. People with externalized consciousness feel empty, even though they have family support and physical comfort. They may also feel that they have achieved little, though they have achieved many things in worldly terms. The human body functions mechanically, obeying the laws of physiology, but the individual is not consciously involved in bodily activities. When the body functions like a machine, people may experience illness and discomfort, though there is nothing wrong with the physical body. When examined medically, they display normal health, yet a sense of discomfort, a perception of loss, a feeling of emptiness prevails. However, there is a way to recover from this state of meaninglessness and apathy.

The first step is to reduce voluntary physical activity. We must bring our bodies to a state of rest. The second step is to synchronize our breathing with the rhythm of our bodies. The third step is to draw the curtains of our eyes in order to separate ourselves from the world and to protect ourselves from worldly temptations. In normal terms, we are merely closing our eyes but, in the spiritual sense, we are silencing the mind and reducing outgoing mental energy, consciously preventing extra brain activity from fatiguing us in response to outside stimuli. Thus we reduce the lavish expenditure of energy, and begin to descend from the ocean surface of the physical body to the depths of the inner being.

In this process, we begin to rediscover ourselves. Awakening our emotions, we are able to tap the power of creativity and unleash latent energy resources. Consistent practice of these steps can result in accessing our great potential. As we move from the surface of the intellectual-consciousness to the intuitive-consciousness of our being we begin to obtain answers and to find solutions. We discover our mystical beauty, rather than concentrating merely on our physical beauty.

Many people believe that being spiritual means withdrawing from the world, staying in solitude and silence, being detached and meditating most of the time. Or they may think dogmatically that we should live austerely, giving up pleasurable activities.

Just as we learn to rediscover and recognize ourselves, we are also able to recognize others and relate to them. We become convinced of our mystical connection or spiritual relationship with everyone, regardless of background. We have realized our connection through the medium of experience, with all that exists.

We are no longer merely worldly or physical in nature; we are more human, more universal and more cosmic. We become increasingly connected with the inner and outer realms of consciousness and sense little difference between others and ourselves. We are connected. Wherever we go, we find friendship and witness love in others. Even extremely negative, materialistic people sense our positive energy and our positive effect, which is conducive to moving their hearts. The process of experiencing various dimensions of our spirit begins with the descent of our consciousness from the mind to the heart, to the core of our being.

If we cannot relate to others, if we keep finding fault with others, if we always have opposing views and conflicts and end up contradicting everyone else, then we have not recognized ourselves. We have not loved ourselves. Others can do physical work for us, but no one can eat for us. When we are thirsty, others cannot quench our thirst by drinking for us. How then can anyone else work for our spiritual growth? We must make the wish: 'I want to expand my consciousness. I want to realize my potential and resources. I want to know my unique nature and purpose in life.' Then the guidance of inspiration descends on us.

29

Inner and Outer Experience

Meditative consciousness

It is possible to be raised to a meditative state of consciousness. When we have acceptance in our hearts, when we have embraced everything in our consciousness without question, doubt or disbelief, and with criticism suspended, then we achieve a meditative form of being.

When we reach a state of innocence, we re-awaken our childhood beauty. We become one with nature. But if we only want to understand our thoughts and feelings on a rational basis, we lose our connection to the heart. We gain little when we merely become engaged in argument with ourselves or with others. However, when we are in a state of silence, accepting all that surrounds our hearts, we gain a great deal. Thus, we understand a situation or an external condition better and are able to bring about the required changes whenever and wherever possible.

Acceptance means becoming one with whatever is happening within us with regard to our thoughts, images or words, and energies. Many people expect change to occur to meet their desired needs before they feel acceptance. But it should be the other way round. First welcome, understand, tune in and then change. Either change personally, or change others or the situation. Acceptance means inviting *everything* into our inner universe. We can compare this phenomenon with an ocean that accepts rivers coming from all directions. The ocean holds enormous treasure. We can access such treasure if we accept our existence. If we accept with complete sincerity the way we are positioned in nature and the universe, a feeling of oneness will be established within us. If we have an aversion to anything, we will not be able to raise ourselves to a meditative state. We have to set aside all differences and accept everything and everyone before we can bring about any type of change. If we are able to accomplish this, then mystical and spiritual experiences will occur within our consciousness.

The spiritual approach is an alternative way of experiencing one's consciousness. A direct approach is through logical thinking and the use of a critical mind. This enables us to understand the truth that is mainly physical. In order to probe the innermost realms of our beings, however, we must use an alternative method – a spiritual approach.

If you want to see the back of your head, you do not simply hold a mirror in front of you. You also have to hold a second mirror at the right angle. Only then can you view the back of your head. Similarly, we need an alternative method to understand ourselves and to experience our spiritual side. We need to do more than use our mind and senses in the physical world. When we want to expand intellectually, we ask questions, we study and we read books. We experiment and debate. We exchange our views, thoughts and concepts with others, and thus our intellect develops. This is part of the expansion of consciousness.

Internal growth requires a different approach. We become observers rather than participants, silent instead of emitting sound. We provide answers instead of generating questions, turning our minds inward by reversing the flow of our outgoing energy and resources. We close our eyes in a meditative state because we want to minimize outgoing energy. While meditating, we may adopt a particular posture, perhaps sitting, standing or reclining. We withdraw ourselves from external action. By responding to our own intuitive signals, we lead ourselves to deeper levels of consciousness.

Each of us understands the outside world in our own way. We create our own beliefs, we postulate our own theories, and thus the world reflects our perceptions. Sometimes we are successful in convincing others to think and believe as we do. Individuals or even entire groups of people may be transformed, though this is not always possible. The energy of transformation remains in them only if we have had in-depth experience of the universe within ourselves. Otherwise the energy and impressions of transformation cannot remain amongst them for a long period of time. Something else will appear to influence them in turn.

When we decide to embark on a journey to experience the spiritual self, we prepare ourselves in many ways. Our decision awakens our intuition. If we follow that intuitive guidance, we are directed to inner experiences.

Individual experience of one's consciousness becomes possible when there is a sincere and personal effort. We can meditate with the aim of fostering someone else's well-being, their spiritual progress or their personal evolution, but each of these must be achieved by the individual. We each progress with our own will and by our own accord, through personal endeavour. Discovering the true self is more intriguing than any other adventure. We are all interested in learning about ourselves and having spiritual experiences, because we have learned over time that nothing is more satisfying than knowing and experiencing one's true self.

We have spent centuries trying to learn about the world we live in, about the planets around us and about nature. We still pursue this quest for knowledge, although it has not brought us inner happiness. What may bring us happiness is that people are becoming more aware of their inner spirituality. This is a good omen for future generations.

As we make scientific and technological advances, we become more spiritual. Our scientific understanding helps us to realize that we are more than we believe ourselves to be. If we explore the depths of our inner being, we will be in touch with the spiritual aspect of the universe.

Diverse paths

Some people believe in life after death. Some believe in reincarnation. Others say that death is the total annihilation of a living entity; nothing follows death. The person who believes that there is no life after death will cease to exist as an individual being after discarding the physical body, and their consciousness will be absorbed into nature's infinitude. The person who believes deeply that there *is* life after death will create the possibility of extending their life far beyond the physical plane of existence. This is the power of will and consciousness. We have the power to do as we wish with our lives and with the self. We all possess that freedom of choice, thought and will, the freedom to reach higher consciousness, and the freedom to be connected to the universal consciousness while existing as individual beings.

Nevertheless, espousing platitudes does not create a reality. Only time-tested, sincere belief, evinced in our hearts, will and consciousness can facilitate our cosmic voyage and transform our existence into what we desire it to be.

Often, in religious practices, individuals can become tuned in to a single thought, a single concept, a single objective or a single belief. The overall focus is on a single source and each individual mind is absorbed into a collective unconscious mind, leading to a dimension of experience, in which anyone who is not 'tuned in' is perceived as being on the wrong path. Such a focusing of belief is described as a cult, and just as those within the cult believe that outsiders are on the wrong path, conversely outsiders think that those within the cult are on the wrong path.

Who is wrong and who is right? Are we able to judge? What is the first question and where can we find an ultimate answer? Some people are ready to die for a cause; their belief system is the basis of their thoughts and actions. We are beings of change. We change physically, psychologically and emotionally. What we accept today we may reject tomorrow and vice versa. However, if a thought, an image or a belief sits deep within in a person's consciousness, it will be reflected in that person's behaviour. No one can change another person's belief until an impression enters that person's consciousness that can act as an antidote to the original impression. The members of cults project their consciousness to a single point, a single focus of understanding, and they become a *body* of consciousness moving in a single direction. The projection of consciousness and will are immensely powerful. Hence, each of us must become aware of his or her unique inner nature. Each of us has to work internally in our own intuitive way, but we must also remain open to receiving inspiration from any source, so that we do not place an inordinate emphasis on individuality. We will then be able to grow and evolve in all possible dimensions, embracing everything around us.

Reflection

An individual has to decide what he or she wants. While some people cannot decide until they are driven by circumstances to make a decision, others take a long time but retain the ability to decide their purpose in life once they are inspired. They want to see themselves in another person or in something in nature. When they find their reflection in some external source, they are reminded of their own purpose. We all need physical, mental and inner reflection. If we do not experience reflection, negative forces have the power to block or hinder our expansion. We then become weak and feeble, and fear dominates us.

We feel elated when someone pays us a compliment or presents us with a gift. We thank them because we see our spiritual reflection. This reflection can also be seen in different aspects of nature.

Suppose that we are alone in a town. We are given the use of all kinds of facilities. We are on our own in that place for a week. There is no one to observe us. We are deliberately alone. However, no matter how much we may enjoy solitude, being alone will bother us after a while. Whether we cry or smile, there is no one to reflect our presence. We have no one with whom to share anything. An eerie negativity surrounds us. We begin to decline.

Searching for truth is the same as searching for our reflection, because we are all blessed with the necessary information and resources to make our lives a celebrated, joyous journey. But we still need reflection. As our consciousness is mainly drawn to the region of the head, we have a tendency to look outside to observe our surroundings. Philosophical study and a spiritual approach help us understand and experience more of the world around us, and help us to elevate our consciousness.

When we cannot find a cure for a physical discomfort, we resort to alternative solutions, whereupon we find some relief. In the same way, in order for us to understand and resolve psychological and emotional complexities, we need an alternative approach that can deepen our awareness and expand our consciousness.

Although we all breathe the same air and live on the same planet, we think, we believe and we act differently. Yet we are all human. We are all particles of pollen in the same cosmic flower of life. There is truth in all forms of existence. When someone says that he or she does not believe, that is a particular perception which may appear senseless or meaningless from the point of view of another. We live as we believe, constructing the book of life out of the impressions and experiences gained by projecting our consciousness. Personal belief becomes the definition of our life. Belief is the launchpad from which human consciousness lifts off into the world of personal realities. Our beliefs are cherished by the conscious mind and nourished by the unconscious.

Searching for truth also means searching for our reflection.

We become spiritually illuminated or enlightened when we embrace various views and experiences, with completely open hearts and minds. Self-awareness can be attained by following spiritual guidelines or by working spiritually, either individually or collectively. But spiritual illumination, the height of consciousness, encompasses all that we discuss and all that we feel and experience. At the height of consciousness, we possess the ability to tune ourselves to any entity in the universe and to relate ourselves to any facet of truth.

We have questions, but we cannot find answers. After a while we give up the search for answers and sit in silence. Then, unexpectedly, answers come. How does this happen? The answers emerge from our own inner consciousness. Perhaps we know the contents of a book before we read it; or we recognize a new place without having visited it before; or we see someone and believe we know them, yet we have never met. This suggests that the inner self is connected to everyone and everything. The self reminds us of this connection by bringing awareness of these experiences to the surface of the mind. Although the connection is strikingly evident, our sceptical mind denies what is really an invitation for us to take a plunge into the vastness of our being, to become more enlightened about our true nature and potential.

When awareness dawned in human beings, there were no printed books for us to read and learn from. We expressed ourselves with gestures, words, song, dance, art and creativity. Now our libraries are filled with books. In the age of information technology, the pace of life is faster than ever. However, too much dependence on technology may induce both physical and mental lethargy. Though we are able to complete our work much more rapidly than ever before, we have become more impatient. A moment waiting at the traffic lights, a few more seconds connecting a telephone call, a few minutes of delay on a plane journey or seconds before the lift arrives and we become anxious, frustrated or disappointed. Our desires are increasing. Everybody wants everyone else's time. We never have enough time to satisfy us.

Our lives are becoming mechanized and every activity is becoming so measured and planned that the opportunity for spontaneity and imagination are decreasing. Our feelings and emotions become shallow because we lack the time to educate them. '*I am very busy,*' appears to be the mantra of the day. There are books that teach step-by-step meditation, how to love one's partner and how to find happiness. These books fail to provide satisfaction as the mechanized instructions they contain contradict human sentiments.

Meditation

Pre-eminently, there are two kinds of meditation. One is thinking meditation and the other is feeling meditation. Thinking meditation involves more complex thinking by asking us to follow specific steps, whereas the feeling meditation deepens our feelings and places less emphasis on rationality. Feeling meditation soaks us in the tender experiences of our hearts. In this state, the mind becomes an accepted, silent source of experience rather than a source of conflict within us.

We are spending a vast amount of time, energy and money promoting digital, analytical rationality as essential to human progress. However, a parallel dedication to peace, love, joy and grace eludes us because it is easier to neglect the needy heart than the greedy mind.

Ignorance cannot totally vanish from our minds, as it exists always at different levels, nor can knowledge totally brighten up our minds. They have to exist in parallel, in different proportions, bringing bliss and joy to our lives.

Meditation is not an alternative to medicine. We cannot meditate without being happy and we cannot be emotionally and spiritually well and at peace without meditation. There is no automatic attainment of a meditative state. Meditation requires preparation. When we are disturbed by our thoughts, we cannot immediately meditate and relieve ourselves of negative energy. The discomfort caused by a negative thought can only be repaired or corrected by another thought that is positive. Only knowledge counteracts ignorance. Corrective knowledge works as an antidote. In eastern philosophy, the state achieved is called *Gnanam*, which can only be attained by people who possess significant spiritual insight. Such people use few words but transmit greater meaning through silence and meditation. When we have embraced everything in our consciousness and sincerely accepted all that is within us and outside us, we too can achieve this state.

30

The Progression to Enlightenment – A Series of Steps

Sunrise and sunset

When the sun rises, darkness disappears. When light is present, darkness is absent. Similarly, when the thinking mind is predominant, the feeling heart subsides. There is no fine line that separates the mind and the heart. The point of balance between these two poles is a place of mystical meditation or is an experience of mysticism, like the experience of twilight. When one's presence is felt deeply in the heart, it is a spiritual experience. When one is fully present in the mind, one is not in the heart, and vice versa. However, darkness and light are both essential for the beauty of life. When we go to extremes, either into the core of darkness or into the very centre of dazzling light, we are blinded. But if we have a choice, we choose light. At least we may be aware of what is occurring around us in blinding light, whereas in darkness, fear of the unknown frightens us and takes our breath away.

Each time we see the sun rising over the eastern horizon, it is as if a new door has opened in our lives, increasing our sense of elation. We love to watch the sunrise. It has a profoundly positive, awakening effect. Conversely, as the sun gradually lowers over the western horizon, we feel serene and settled. We enter into a state of bliss. One state of mind is the effect of sunrise, while the other is the effect of sunset.

The amalgamation of light and darkness is in equal proportions at both sunrise and sunset. But the effects are different. The morning sun invites us to dwell more in the mind, and to experience the sounds of the day and the world. The evening sun creates an atmosphere of serenity and inspires us to experience the beauty of nature in our hearts. We are strongly influenced by the outside environment. Thus, we raise the sun of our consciousness to our minds with the rising of the sun outside and we become inspired to bring our consciousness down to our hearts with the setting of the sun.

With the rays of the sun we raise our consciousness to our egotistic minds and with the setting of the sun we descend with our consciousness to our humble hearts.

Before taking on our present state, we existed in some form somewhere in the universe. Whether we consider ourselves as mere matter or energy, or consciousness, or something else, only the *forms* of our existence change.

Just as we exist in the present, we manifested ourselves in infinite variety in the past. There are traces of us in nature and in the universe of our past. Only a few discover and access these traces and such people can feel lonelier than others, because there is no one with whom they can share their experiences. If they do attempt to express themselves, their experiences are viewed as frenetic or bizarre. Those who are able to access other manifestations of themselves are often dismissed as being mentally out of balance.

Sometimes it is better to be ordinary than special. If we become too special, we are excluded from the world unless we use our special qualities with humility. For example, being wealthy need not be just a matter of earning money. We need to know how to save, protect and maintain our wealth while keeping our egos in check and working at running our businesses. We should work with the rest of our staff as one among them, acknowledging the qualities in others, instead of feeling superior ourselves. If we remain humble, we achieve greatness. Then we evince a humility and simplicity that is complemented by pride and dynamism.

Similarly, it is not enough to gain an insight into our previous forms of existence, to learn about them and experience them. What is important is the extent to which we can absorb and assimilate those impressions into our *present* state of existence. How much we listen to the discoveries, insights and experiences of others and help them to relate to us is also very important. If we learn to incorporate the experiences of others along with our own, we will have entered the nearly impenetrable, sacred realms of nature.

Sound and silence

To access the data of pre-existence, we have to silence the mind, that is, the surface mind. Then the deeper mind awakens and takes us to the intuitive heart. Silence becomes more and more profound as we descend into the depths of consciousness. Of course, outer silence must be synchronized with inner silence. We have the tendency to be silent if we are upset, disturbed or exhausted. Silence allows us to revive and recharge our spirits before returning to the chaotic world. We cannot make good decisions while being bombarded by sound. A noisy atmosphere impels us to action, but major decisions are best made in an atmosphere of silence. This does not mean that such decisions will always be perfect, but with silence we can minimize untoward results.

We were silent before we entered this plane of existence; and we will again go into periods of silence, only to emerge into the same or another form of existence, here or elsewhere, in the infinite ocean of cosmic consciousness.

There is no action without sound and there is no sound without action. When a particle collides with another particle, there is an emanation of subtle vibrations. When a planet or star collides with another celestial object, it produces an enormous explosion. We do not hear this partly because it is too far away and partly because of the vacuum that separates us from it.

The universe manifests itself in the emanation of sounds from the silence of cosmic consciousness. Sound and action will coexist as long as the universe exists. Every action is followed by a sound of contact, an explosion or collision. Our auditory nerves and our minds are provided with intense stimulation by a plethora of sounds. We are bombarded, especially in these modern times, by sound pollution adding to the sensitivity of our health and of the environment.

Silence is not much appreciated by the mind. The mind requires constant stimulation, otherwise it ceases to function properly. When we close our eyes without spiritual inspiration or interest, we feel lethargic, because we have greatly reduced the stimuli busying our minds.

The mind is an extended entity of the inner consciousness. It exists on the surface. It is a connecting agent between the senses, the body and the memory centre. Inner consciousness blossoms and spreads itself all around the being when there is a serene uplifting atmosphere.

Suppose we attempt the following experiment. We travel to a village or into the mountains, or anywhere nature prevails without urban interruption. We feel something special, something fulfilling, though there is nothing present to entertain us. We do not know what it is. In actuality it is nature's silence and serenity that is inspiring us. The inner consciousness of the self blossoms in the sunlight of beauty and silence. If we simply close our eyes in that situation, we will be bathed in the bliss of silence, joy and serenity, which change our inner spirits.

The true nature of inner consciousness is silence. The true nature of the mind is sound. The mind is like an extension of the deeper consciousness. We may refer to the mind as a bubble of consciousness. Or we may call it the face of consciousness. But the mind does not represent the whole of consciousness.

The head, where the face and most of the senses are seated, is often the first part of the body to be noticed; thus the mind is volatile and very sensitive, excited by thousands of stimuli every second. It is difficult to quieten the mind. Silence, on the other hand, can be felt in one's heart since it is an organ that is placed almost at the centre of the body and is well protected by the ribs and muscles. Future science will evolve faster and become revolutionized because of its openness and an increased capacity to accommodate many possible ways of approaching physical facts and the sensitive truths of metaphysics. Future scientists will not hesitate to incorporate their personal experiences into their impersonal methods of studying and researching. They will acknowledge that the heart is the mother of mind. Then further research will seek the location of the heart in our body and our consciousness. The threshold of that research will be the cardiovascular heart.

It is from the heart that all noble qualities emerge.

The mind is like an office and the heart is like a home. There can be discipline in the mind but the heart feels love. We do not love from the mind. We love from the heart. Love should be distinguished from lust, which is experienced through the senses, and directed by the nervous system. Experience that is only lustful is not deep. We forget it after a time, whereas the experience of love leaves a lasting impression and is not easily forgotten. Whether the expression of love is a word, a look, a touch, a smile or just the presence of a person, it is remembered forever, because this memory is both subtle and deep, an experience that is not yet understood by the medical world.

Enlightenment and human will

Some people believe that everything in life is predetermined. If this were true, life would be meaningless. We would not be responsible for our actions and their consequences. The superbly creative intelligent forces that are responsible for the universe also made us feel responsible by bestowing upon us individual will and freedom of choice, so that we can attain fulfilment in life. The will is like the steering system of a car. When we make choices, we are manifesting our will. The will is an operational device that is invisible, internal and highly mystical. Others can only give us instructions or suggestions, but we are the operators. We can project our consciousness in any direction, into any dimension. We can descend within ourselves or heighten our being. We are steering ourselves by applying our will. If we do this within the disciplines of the universe and creation, we can progress and evolve materialistically and spiritually. We can use meditation to enhance our willpower.

As we journey deeper, we begin to evolve in many aspects. Consciousness expands, encircling us like an energy field, and our vision becomes clearer. The distance from the head to the heart is only a few centimetres. But the mystical journey to expansion of consciousness is a life-long blossoming process in its beauty and spirituality.

The moment that one's cursor-like awareness (surface consciousness – in the head) reaches the core conscious Self, as steered by one's will, there is a brilliant opening and awakening in the whole being. This is the mystical experience of the illumination of the true Self. Enlightenment takes us a step closer to reaching the outer Self, which is infinitely sensitive, subtle and macrocosmic. Enlightenment penetrates everything. When consciousness is intensified through personal endeavour and sincere internal persuasion, it is possible to reach the heart of the cosmos or the very core of cosmic conscious laws. *Expanded consciousness leads one to higher understanding of the universe and its relationship with one's inner self.* This is the state of enlightenment. Enlightened people understand the secrets of universal communication and the art of managing and varying their energy levels and of absorbing energy from various sources in the universe. They can connect with elements in nature, accessing higher information that pertains to the well-being of humankind.

We all wish to be perfect. Many of us wish to achieve enlightenment, but something prevents us from attaining this goal; negative forces cause us to deviate from our own humanity. In addition, we are distracted from the path of enlightenment by problems such as ageing, pain, disease and death, as well as by weaknesses of the mind.

We can change the way these distractions affect us only if change is within the scope of our will. Even then, change is not always possible. The mind rarely accepts this, since denial is the overpowering nature of the mind. But the heart accepts, forgives, shows compassion and endures. When we accept things that cannot be changed, then we open up a new dimension of unimagined possibilities. We become unified with the forces of nature. We are then able to effect some remarkable changes in our thinking, our feelings, our whole personality and the magnitude of our understanding and experience of life.

Some of us may already have been enlightened, but we just need to recognize this. Some may be far away from being enlightened but they have their own time in which to attain enlightenment. Some have embarked on the path of enlightenment. Some are truly enlightened.

Glossary of Terms

Ananda: a Sanskrit term to describe an elated state of consciousness, where there is a high degree of joy

Atman: a Sanskrit term for soul, spirit, conscious self or pure spiritual entity

Buddha: 'enlightened one' in Sanskrit. Buddha was born in southern Nepal and lived 563–483 BC. He achieved enlightenment at the age of 35 and is renowned throughout the world for his spiritual doctrines

Collective consciousness: the state of consciousness of all beings, which exists collectively

Consciousness: the state of being conscious, being in one's senses and aware of one's surroundings; mental activity that includes emotion and thought. Deep-seated consciousness impels human beings to search for truth, love, meaning and deeper experiences. Consciousness is the individual operating with awareness, deeper consciousness not being readily accessible to our own conscious mind unless we make an individual effort by reducing the surface activities of the conscious mind

Dhyana: an experience of spontaneous intuitive meditation that occurs in oneself after one embarks on an inner journey, having been inspired by nature, the universe or a spiritually evolved person

Energy fields: waves of energy that are emitted by, and surround, each being. Energy fields, composed in part of human experiences and memories, form a mystical circle, also known as an aura, around a person

Externalization: the projection of the consciousness into the external world, with the use of the mind's logic and rationality; exploration and realization of the outer universe

Galactic dark matter: dark matter, which makes up 90% of the total mass of a typical galaxy; also referred to as GDM. While GDM absorbs energy, it does not radiate; physicists still do not fully understand GDM

Gnanam: a Sanskrit term meaning corrective knowledge – intuitive, philosophical and spiritual – which works as an antidote to ignorance or confusion; *gnanam* can be attained by people with significant spiritual insight; they are capable of transmitting great meaning through silence, through words or with their presence

Heart: Just as the physical heart, which pumps blood around the body, and the brain are contrasted with each other in their structure, function and effects, so the physical brain can be understood somewhat separately from the mind and the spiritual heart can be felt differently from the physical heart

Inner space: in analogy with the physical space outside our being, concentrated mystical space within the feeling heart and consciousness

Internalization: the process of focusing one's consciousness and energies on the internal world, through silence, feeling, intuition and graceful concentration on the non-physical self; exploration and realization of the inner universe

Meditation (1): consists of (a) thinking meditation, which involves complex thinking in solitude, being deeply focused on a subject, where the emphasis is on logic and rationality, later emerging with brilliant clarity, and (b) feeling meditation, which deepens the feelings and places less emphasis on rationality; the mind being a silent, accepted source of experience, leading oneself into the heart

Meditation (2): attainment of a heightened state of consciousness, which is not automatic and requires preparation through silence, patience, discipline and withdrawal from the external world, to focus energy and consciousness within

Metaphysics: the branch of philosophy that deals with spirituality and mysticism; it includes ontology and cosmology and is used here to refer to a knowledge beyond physics

Mind: a by-product of consciousness and an entity extended from the deeper consciousness; the mind is the seat of logic and rationality, a gateway into the world of illusions and emotions

Mystic gestures: these transmit the deeper intended meaning a person wishes to convey through his or her hands and eyes; they alter the state of consciousness in both the person who expresses the gestures and the person who observes or receives them

Pragna: the Sanskrit term for consciousness

Reflection: consists of physical reflection, mental reflection and inner reflection; it is through reflection that the purpose and uniqueness of individuals is discovered and, through it, mystical insights can be achieved after the seeker experiences the reflection of their inner being in another person or in nature

Sadhana: the Sanskrit term for personal endeavour for spiritual growth for potential enlightenment, where one is almost always consciously aware of one's spiritual development

Self: the true Self can be discovered with consistent effort, determination and dedication, and as a result of inspiration by those who are spiritually evolved; the true Self exists at a deeper and more profound level than the surface Self of ego and 'I-ness'. Self means the core, the essential being of one's existence

Spirit-consciousness: at the beginning and end stages of life, spirit-consciousness is in its purest form; consciousness is the effect of one's spirit dwelling in the physical body; consciousness and spirit reflect each other, creating multiple opportunities in each person for memory, creativity and imagination

Surface-mind consciousness: a state of consciousness where awareness of self and spiritual inquiry are on the surface or at the level of the mind only, without deeper feelings of the heart, intuition and consciousness-awareness